TIMELESS NEEDS, ETERNAL HOPE

Wanda Lutrell is a desperate woman. And truth be told—so are you and I. We are overcommitted, overtired, and overwhelmed. We are busy women with deep needs, broad concerns, and high hopes. In this unpredictable world, we are reminded to present these needs and hopes to God. Our sisters in Scripture did the very same thing and we have much to learn from their faith as well as their foibles. Wanda deftly weaves the stories of biblical women, fairy-tale characters, and real-life modern women into a vibrant tapestry that will touch you on a very personal level. *Timeless Needs, Eternal Hope* will encourage you to step out in faith like sisters from our past and to diligently and desperately seek God concerning our future. Hope awaits you!

—**ELLIE LOFARO,** BIBLE TEACHER, SPEAKER, AUTHOR OF *LEAP OF FAITH* AND *FROM BATTLE SCARS TO BEAUTY MARKS*

Wanda's book is evidence that we women throughout the ages are not so different. Don't we wish we knew more about Mrs. Job, or the Prodigal's mother, or the Innkeeper's wife from Bethlehem? Their stories might mirror our own. Maybe our heartbreaks, failures, and triumphs are just like theirs. Maybe their struggles, yearnings, and discoveries are much like our own. In this wonderful book, Wanda Luttrell takes us on a journey of hope and inspiration, as we see how God sees and answers the heart cry of his women—in ancient times as well as today.

—**NANCY STAFFORD,** ACTRESS *(MATLOCK)*, SPEAKER, AND AUTHOR OF *THE WONDER OF HIS LOVE: A JOURNEY INTO THE HEART OF GOD* AND *BEAUTY BY THE BOOK: SEEING YOURSELF AS GOD SEES YOU*

The author of *Timeless Needs, Eternal Hope* asks, "What do you need today?" Is it mercy? Courage? Hope? Whatever drives your desperate search, this book helps you find comfort in calling out to God with the assurance he will hear you. Drawing from Scripture and a wealth of life experiences, Wanda Luttrell offers readers sensitive encouragement and biblical answers in times of trouble.

—**LIZABETH DUCKWORTH,** AUTHOR OF
BLOOM BEFORE YOU'RE PLANTED AND *WILDFLOWER LIVING*

Grab a coffee, nestle up in an armchair, and let Wanda show you how to cope with life and how to accept God's forgiveness.

—**ANDREW SNADEN,** AUTHOR OF *WHEN GOD MET A GIRL*

TIMELESS
needs
ETERNAL
hope

TIMELESS
needs
ETERNAL
hope

*Let the Lives of Biblical Women
Speak to Your Desperate Heart*

WANDA LUTTRELL

LIFE JOURNEY®
Bringing Home the Message for Life

COOK COMMUNICATIONS MINISTRIES
Colorado Springs, Colorado • Paris, Ontario
KINGSWAY COMMUNICATIONS LTD
Eastbourne, England

Life Journey® is an imprint of
Cook Communications Ministries, Colorado Springs, CO 80918
Cook Communications, Paris, Ontario
Kingsway Communications, Eastbourne, England

TIMELESS NEEDS, ETERNAL HOPE
© 2007 by Wanda Luttrell

Cover Design: The DesignWorks Group
Cover Photo: © Anthony Richards/ Trevillion Images

First Printing, 2007
Printed in the United States of America

1 2 3 4 5 6 7 8 9 10 / 11 10 09 08 07

ISBN 978-0-7814-4484-2
LCCN 2007929474

For Elizabeth Barnett Moore—my stepmother, my mentor, my friend—who has loved me as her own and shared so much that "we will not forget."

In loving memory of her son and my brother, Darrell Scott Moore, whose story appears in the Job's Wife chapter of this book.

Special thanks to Mike Nappa, Nappaland Literary Agency, without whose creative suggestions this book never would have been written. Thanks, Mike!

CONTENTS

INTRODUCTION

*D*esperate situations seem to follow my family like swarms of mosquitoes. If we are not currently in one, we have just come out of one or are getting ready to go into one.

For example, a few weeks ago we were desperate because the fan quit working on my car's heater/air-conditioner; the window on the driver's side lowered, then would not go back up, and it was raining; my daughter had job interviews and no one to watch the kids; and my editor wanted major changes in a manuscript with a looming deadline. To top it all off, I went out to feed the cats and found that some "kind soul" had dropped off a seventh cat, a hungry, forlorn little female who would need immediate surgery if I didn't want a litter of kittens.

A few months ago we were desperate because of real emergencies.

While I was keeping vigil at a hospital where my brother lay dying of cancer, my husband suffered a major heart attack in another state several hours away. He had to have a stent put in one artery immediately. One daughter drove me there while one flew in from out of state, and another struggled to get a plane ticket home from out of the country. While we were away, my brother died, and we had to rush back for the funeral, with my husband needing a second stent as soon as it could be scheduled back home. Meanwhile, my son broke his right hand the day before he was to report to work at a new job.

I would guess that you can identify with desperation like this and with some of the women in this book—those taken from the Bible as well as their modern-day counterparts. I have chosen the stories for this book because each one will help you see a different aspect of how God cares for desperate women—these women, as well as you and me.

I've prepared the stories of desperate biblical characters with a bit of reading between the lines and imaginative scene-setting.

Some of the modern stories you will read are so candid that I've changed names and a few of the circumstances to protect the characters' privacy. But the stories all are based on true events.

While writing these accounts of women who found themselves in distressing situations, I began to see that when a desperate woman draws on God's strength and wisdom, instead of trying to work things out on her own, she doesn't have to remain desperate. A widow has her financial and emotional needs met miraculously. A prodigal's despairing mother finds hope. A pregnant teenager finds strength to do what is right. A woman with low self-esteem is raised to a new level. A forsaken sinner finds grace.

As you read these accounts of ordinary women caught up in extraordinary events, I pray you will realize you can call out to God in any circumstance and he will hear your cry.

1

BATHSHEBA

THEME: *forgiveness*

Scripture: 2 Samuel 11–12

S he grabbed a small napkin from the kitchen table and ran out the back door, her stomach heaving as she ran.

Parting company with my breakfast has become an everyday occurrence these days, she thought, wiping her mouth on the napkin. *What's wrong with me?* she cried silently. But she knew. It had been two months since she had seen evidence of her womanhood. The condition she had longed for from the beginning of her marriage was upon her.

I am with child, Bathsheba thought in despair, *and my husband has not been near me since he went to fight the Ammonites with King David's army.* The flowers in the garden had not even begun to bud when he left. Now they were spent, their blossoms brown, their leaves shriveled in the merciless sun.

They had wanted a child, but the joy of parenthood had been denied them for some reason by *Yahweh.* Now this experience that would have brought such joy in other circumstances only caused her grief and despair.

"What am I to do?" she whispered. "I am with child by the king." There could be no other explanation. There had been no others. She never had been unfaithful to Uriah before, had not even considered such a thing. She had taken seriously the commandments she heard read from the Torah as she listened from the Court of Women. One of them said plainly, "You shall not commit adultery."

What could I have done, Adonai? she anguished. *I had no choice but to obey the king. Or did I?*

Her thoughts flew back to that warm spring night, heavy with the scent of grape bloom and the cry of the turtledove from the palace gardens. The dark velvet sky had been filled with stars so near that she felt she could reach out and touch them as she bathed on her rooftop in their luminous glow, unaware of watching eyes.

King David had seen her bathing, he said, and her body had excited him as no other ever had. Bathsheba felt a remnant of the guilty pride those words had brought her that night. Despite the many wives and concubines whose sole purpose was to bring him pleasure, the handsome king wanted her.

She hadn't wanted to betray her sweet Uriah. He had been a good and gentle husband since the day he had brought her as his bride to this lovely little house at the edge of the palace grounds. Never had she had to glean behind the reapers, as her elder sister had done to feed her numerous children. Never had she borne the shame of bruises and blackened eyes as her younger sister so often wore when her brute of a husband was inspired by the demons of fermented wine.

Uriah loved her better than his own life. He was a faithful and honorable husband. She was as sure of that as she was of the fact that she had committed adultery against him. Hot shame flushed her skin. She dipped her fingers in the basin of the fountain and patted lukewarm water over her face and neck, fighting another wave of nausea that swept over her like the hot summer breeze.

Her pale face looked back at her, reflected in the water of the basin, and she stared at the dark circles shadowing her once-bright dark eyes. She had gone from a contented, attractive young woman to this haggard-looking thing—all because of that one night she had spent at the palace.

"But he is the king," she said aloud. "How could I refuse him? He is the supreme ruler of Israel!"

The memory of that one incredible night filled her mind, and another hot flush of shame swept over her. If she had pleaded with him not to make her violate her marriage vows to one of his most faithful soldiers, would he have honored her request? He had been so ardent, so convinced of his right to whatever he desired.

Yet, in all honesty, had not the king's intense desire inflamed her own emotions, starved since her husband had gone with the army to Rabbah those many weeks ago? Had she not felt desire for this handsome, virile monarch who wanted her above all others?

Bathsheba fanned her hot face with the hem of her garment. She could not honestly say she had been raped. Mentally, she might have been forced, but physically, her own body had betrayed her.

And now here I am with child by the king of Israel, she thought, *for whom Uriah risks his life daily. Oh,* haShem, *what have I done?* Whatever the circumstances, she knew she was guilty of betraying one of the finest men in Israel.

Uriah was a Hittite by birth, but his service to King David was as devoted as that of any natural-born son of Israel. He brought much honor to the uniform he wore with pride.

She had been drawn to him that first day he had stood before her in the market, asking the price of a slab of goat cheese. He was not such a handsome man, but he had the muscular build of a disciplined soldier, and he walked with the dignity of wisdom gained from a decade of living beyond her own few years.

Above all, she had seen a kindness in his soft gray eyes as he paid the price she named for the cheese without bargaining. Somehow he had known she needed the sale to avert her father's anger when she came home at the end of another hot, dusty day in the fickle marketplace.

She hadn't been "in love" with Uriah when her father gleefully announced the deal he had made with the soldier for his middle daughter, but she had accepted the news, if not with joy, with contentment and gratitude. Somehow she had sensed he would be a kind and considerate husband, and such candidates for the hand of a middle daughter with a slim dowry were scarce.

As the years passed, Uriah's kindness and noble character caused her to grow to love him. He was a rare, precious jewel of a man who loved her with all his heart, who supplied her every want eagerly, often before she even knew what she wanted.

"And now I must destroy him," she moaned. "Oh, *Adonai*, please show me what to do!"

As she turned back toward the house, an idea began to grow in her mind, as surely as the unfortunate child grew in her womb. She would go to the king and tell him. Perhaps he would have some suggestion, some power to change this terrible situation.

Bathsheba stirred the hot, still night air with the fan of feathers Uriah had brought her from one of his earlier campaigns. As last night, she had bathed—no longer on the rooftop, but in her secret chamber—and doused herself with a light flower scent. The slight swell of her abdomen was hardly noticeable, she thought gratefully, as she slipped into her best gown and arranged her dark hair in waves around her shoulders. *If only Uriah would come home tonight, as the king promised.*

The king had told her not to worry, that he would take care of everything. Then, yesterday morning, he had sent word that he had called Uriah home from Rabbah to give an account of the battle, and he would be home to sleep with her that night. Perhaps, she had thought, her trusting husband would not count the time between the birth of the child and his visit home. She did not want to deceive Uriah, but maybe he would be so happy to have a child at last that he …

But Uriah had not come to her last night. She had heard from the servants that he had spent last night in the palace gateway with the king's servants, refusing to seek the comfort of his wife's bed while his comrades in arms slept in the fields.

The king had sent word again this morning that she must not lose patience—that he would send her husband to her tonight, filled with wine from the king's table and in a mellow and loving mood.

She knew in her heart that Uriah would not come. As on the night before, no matter how drunk the king tried to get him, this honorable man would not take advantage of the opportunity to sleep with his wife while his fellow soldiers slept alone on the hard ground.

The stars were fading, and only a pale sliver of moon remained to mark the night in the sky. Soon, the sun would spread its glare over the land, and the opportunity to hide her sin would evaporate with the morning dew.

"Oh, Holy One of Israel, what am I to do?" she moaned. "I am guilty, but Uriah is innocent. Honorable. Noble. Must I thrust the cruel confession of my betrayal into his heart like a sword of the Ammonites?" Yet she knew she must confess her sin and take her punishment.

What will Uriah do? she wondered. *Will he give me a writing of divorcement as, according to the Law, he has every right to do because of my uncleanness? Will he send me and my unborn child back to my father?* But she knew there would be no welcome for her there. She could easily imagine her father slamming the door in her face.

She also could imagine the terrible pain that would migrate across Uriah's eyes and settle in their soft gray depths when she admitted her guilt to him. But, try as she would, she could not imagine him sending her away. After a moment of stunned disbelief, he most likely would take her in his arms, kiss her on the top of her head, and tell her that it was not her fault.

When the child came, she knew Uriah would be quite capable of welcoming it as his own, accepting it as a miracle from *Yahweh* to fill the empty void of their barrenness.

The king had whispered in her ear that night that he wished she was not married so he could make her his wife. But no matter how much her carnal nature was attracted to him, she knew she did not want to be a new addition to the king's harem, like a new mare in the stables.

All she wanted was to stay here with Uriah in this pleasant little house, to know the contentment she had known with him before her command performance with the king.

"Oh, Holy One of Israel," she mourned, "will I ever know such contentment again?" If only she could cause time to retreat back to the day before the king had summoned her. If only she could rip out of her life that one night of adultery and return once more to innocence.

JUSTINE

It has been twenty-some years ago now, but I still grieve for the young girl I will call Justine. Her parents were decent people who raised their children in the church and tried to give them every advantage an ordinary, lower-middle-class family could provide. Justine was the youngest, a lovely sprite of a girl with a whole lifetime ahead of her.

Just after her sixteenth birthday, Justine's parents dropped her off at the high school gymnasium door and gave her enough money to buy her ticket to the basketball game and something to eat. Promising to pick her up after the game, they went to a nearby restaurant for dinner.

During dinner Mom felt a darkness come over her spirit. She was convinced that something was wrong with Justine, that she might be ill. She tried to keep her feelings to herself until her husband had finished his meal. However, her spirit became so troubled that she knew she had to go check on her daughter.

They raced back to the high school and found Justine stumbling through the parking lot. When they called to her, she came over to their car, then burst into tears. As they drove home, the sordid story poured out between sobs.

Recently, Justine had begun to experiment with alcohol illicitly provided by her friends from their parents' liquor cabinets. She liked the freedom from inhibitions it gave her and was excited about the sophistication she felt at sampling what she felt was the real adult world.

That night, she had left the ball game with a group of teenage friends and a twenty-one-year-old driver. Flush with hot dog and soda money, she offered to finance the purchase of some bourbon.

As Justine eagerly sampled the fiery liquid, the twenty-one-year-old drove back to the high school and dropped off the others. He refused to let Justine out of the car, and by then, she was too intoxicated to resist. He took her to an isolated spot and raped her as she passed in and out of consciousness.

After a night of recriminations and remorseful tears, the family fell into bed in exhaustion, deciding to wait until the next day to seek medical advice.

That next bleak morning, as Mom prepared a hasty breakfast, Justine sat at the kitchen table listlessly fingering some children's books she had impulsively picked up on her way downstairs.

"'Johnny-Go-Round is a tan tomcat. Would you like to know why we call him that?'" she read aloud.

On and on she read to the end of that story and through several other old favorites, stopping to laugh hollowly at all the familiar places where they always had laughed together. "Humpty-Dumpty sat on the wall ...'"

My heart still aches for the delightful child we had known, now struggling frantically to recapture her lost childhood.

Like Bathsheba longing to turn time back to the day before her adulterous moment with the king, like Eve standing outside the garden wishing she could return to those idyllic moments before she met the snake, Justine sat reading childhood stories, seeking to return to the not-so-long-ago days of innocence, now beyond reach forever.

UNDERSTANDING BATHSHEBA

To understand Bathsheba's part in the story, we have to understand the typical role of a woman in her place and time. A girl grew up in her father's house and lived there until she was old enough to be married off to a man of her father's choice. Then she went to her husband's house to live under his rule as long as he lived.

Even the Wife of Noble Character of Proverbs 31:10–31, who managed a successful home-based business, did so under the approval of her husband. Verses 11 and 12 say, "Her husband has full confidence in her and lacks nothing of value. She brings him good, not harm, all the days of her life." No wonder he praised her as he sat among the elders of the land at the city gates!

If a woman remained unmarried, the best she could hope for at her father's death was to be given a home by whichever male relative inherited her father's property. In the few instances where daughters inherited from their father's estates (e.g., Job's second set of daughters), it was so unusual as to rate a special mention in the Bible.

In Bathsheba's day it was all about men. No wonder Bathsheba felt she had no choice but to obey the king's summons. He not only was a man with the traditional male role of dominance in her life, he was the king. What might he have done if she had refused to come to the palace, if she had rejected his advances?

WHAT IF?

We could play endless games of *what if* here. *What if* Bathsheba had risked the king's ire and ignored his summons? *What if* she had gone to the palace and convinced David not to commit this sin against her marriage vows, against one of his most faithful soldiers?

What if David had ordered her to have an abortion? Midwives had their methods, even back then.

What if Uriah had obeyed David's urgings to go home, had slept with his wife, and, later, knowingly or unknowingly, raised the child as his own? Would Bathsheba have lived happily-ever-after with her husband and her firstborn son in the little cottage outside the palace grounds?

What if Justine had refused to leave the ball game and instead had spent her money on hot dogs and soda? Would she have been able to make wiser choices when the next opportunity to dabble in the grown-up world came her way?

What if Eve—at the beginning of time—had said, "No thank you," to the snake? Would we all still be experiencing the bliss of Eden?

We will never know the answers to those questions. The choices were made, and each choice began an inexorable journey toward an unavoidable conclusion.

UNPREMEDITATED SIN

There's no use agonizing over why Humpty-Dumpty was on the wall in the first place. (Had he been laid there by the mother hen? Had he been placed there temporarily by some careless hand and forgotten? Had the Easter Bunny placed him there for the egg hunt?) He certainly hadn't crawled out there on his own so he could fall. He hadn't intended to become a scrambled egg.

Regardless, he was in the wrong place at the wrong time, and now he lay in pieces on the ground—shell shattered, yolk and white scrambled into a sticky mess that all the king's horses and all the king's men could never put back together again.

None of our three desperate ladies deliberately set out to separate themselves from God. Neither did I. Probably, you didn't either. We had other reasons for making the decisions that led us into sin. Our circumstances, our emotions, our hormones, our desires betrayed us.

Eve wanted to be like God. Bathsheba felt she had little choice but to obey the king. Justine thought she could handle the adult world. Then, the next thing they knew, they had crossed the bridge, and it had burned behind them. They were unable to change the fateful circumstances they had set in motion. They never could return to the innocence they once had known.

Eve bore her children in pain and sorrow, helping her mate scratch a living from the reluctant ground. Bathsheba lived as one of the wives in David's stable, aware that a kind and gentle man had died to allow her this privilege. Justine struggled for years with bitterness and low self-esteem, knowing that, while the rape was someone else's sin, her own bad choices had set the stage.

FINDING GOD'S FORGIVENESS

Perhaps we are all Christians here. We have walked that bridge back to fellowship with God that he created after Eve's defection.

We have acknowledged that we are sinners in need of salvation and have accepted the substitutionary death of God's Son as the answer to that need. We have asked him to come into our lives and be Lord of all we are and have.

But uh-oh. That last sin slipped up on me after I was back in the family. What do I do now? Jeremiah 15:19 says, "*If you repent, I will restore you that you may serve me.*" First John 1:9 promises, "*If we confess our sins,* he is faithful and just and will forgive us our sins and purify us from all unrighteousness."

It took me awhile, though, to realize that these promises are not fulfilled automatically. As with all God's promises, I must comply with prerequisites before I am granted forgiveness. I must truly repent of the sin, confess it to God, and abandon it. Then I am forgiven. The formula is: *Repentance + Confession = God's Forgiveness.*

FORGIVING OURSELVES

I am generous in my acceptance of sincerely repented wrongdoing on the part of others. You probably are, too. We hug the young unwed mother and bring her baby clothes. We pardon the thief, even the murderer whose mother did not love him. We share our pew with the reformed prostitute and invite her to women's ministry activities.

However, just as we expect our children to behave better than the neighbors' children, we expect more of ourselves than we do of others. "I should have had (fill in the blanks) _____ (better sense, more self-control, more character, stricter morals)." "I have failed my (you name it) _____ (spouse, family, friends, church, Lord)." We will not tolerate such failure on our own part. We are convinced we should be better than that. We find it difficult to forgive ourselves for the things we've done wrong.

BEEN THERE? DONE THAT?

One of my greatest sins was a sin of omission. I had been meaning to move my grandmother in with us, into the small house we had built on land she gave us. We were crowded, though, with two people already in each bedroom. I wanted to build on a room for her, but the money just wasn't available.

With living space so limited, I worried about the effect on our children of grandmother's senility. In the three years since my grandfather had died, she had become increasingly angry and confused. She even encouraged one of our teenage daughters in a totally unacceptable relationship, apparently confusing our objections to this seedy character with her own mother's objections to my grandfather because he was older than she and from humble circumstances.

Then the unspeakable happened. Grandmother caught her sweater sleeve on fire as she reached over a hot electric burner to get her coffee pot one morning. She had the good sense to remove her burning clothes and throw them outside, but the damage was done.

As I listened to her screams as the medical staff tried to clean her burns, I watched her slip away from us. I knew my intentions to be there for her—as she always had been for me—had gone up in smoke. I would never be able now to show her how much I appreciated all she had done for me.

I certainly didn't intend to let my grandmother burn to death, but I could not forgive myself for letting her live alone too long. Whatever my reasons, I was guilty of a sin of omission that had horrible, irrevocable consequences.

My unending self-recrimination placed me squarely in the crowded boat with Eve, Bathsheba, and Justine. Like King David, when he was confronted with his sin (2 Sam. 12:13), I knew I was guilty, guilty, guilty. I desperately sought God's forgiveness.

"I believe God has forgiven me," I finally cried, "but I can't forgive myself!"

As I continued scourging myself for my sin, the Holy Spirit got the message through to me that I was not being humble. Instead I was saying arrogantly, "God may be able to forgive me, but my standards are higher than his, and I won't forgive myself."

THE OLD GUILT TRIP

Sometimes we try to deal with our feelings of guilt by denying them. *It wasn't me, Lord. It was that snake you made. He told me to eat that fruit.*

Or we may try to excuse it. *But he is the king, Lord. What could I do?*

We may try to bury it in the forgetfulness of alcohol or pills. *If I just stay drunk or high, I won't remember what I did.*

Sometimes we try to cover it with distractions. *If I surround myself with enough music, TV, people, busyness, noise, I won't be able to think about it.*

We may even make a pet of guilt, feed it, coax it to stay with us. *Guilt makes me feel better, like I've made a down payment for my sin. If I feel guilty enough, I won't commit this sin again.*

Actually, guilt is a warning light that tells us something needs fixing. It does not change us. No matter how guilty we may feel, we are still the same people who made the errors in judgment that got us into trouble in the first place. Worse, we are likely to make the same mistake again—and again. It is the grace of God that changes us. If we truly understand God's grace, we no longer feel guilty. We just feel grateful.

"Therefore, there is now *no condemnation* for those who are in Christ Jesus," Romans 8:1–2 says, "because through Christ Jesus the law of the Spirit of life set me free from the law of sin and death."

God's forgiveness is instant, free, and repeated, if need be, as Nehemiah declared: "You are a God of forgiveness, always ready to pardon, gracious and merciful ... full of love" (Neh. 9:17 TLB). In other words, if you have confessed your sin and asked for forgiveness, God is not mad at you anymore.

REALLY? ARE YOU SURE?

Positive. The blood of Jesus has covered your sins and mine.

They are buried in the deepest sea. ("You will tread our sins underfoot and hurl all our iniquities into the depths of the sea" [Mic. 7:19].)

They are far away. ("As far as the east is from the west, so far has he removed our transgressions from us" [Ps. 103:12].)

God has a short memory. ("For I will forgive their wickedness and will remember their sins no more" [Heb. 8:12].)

Yes, you did wrong. So did I. Yes, God was displeased about that. BUT—we repented, we confessed, and WE ARE FORGIVEN.

BACK TO BATHSHEBA

The Messiah, the Lamb of God who takes away the sin of the world (John 1:29), had not yet appeared in Bathsheba's day, but each year, on Yom Kippur (Day of Atonement), the priest sacrificed an offering to roll those sins forward until the Messiah could come and make the final sacrifice (Lev. 16).

Did Bathsheba know the price of her sin would be paid by the Messiah? Did she realize she could receive God's forgiveness? Samuel doesn't tell us much more about her other than that she was the mother of Solomon (2 Sam. 12:24–25). We can only hope her story continued something like this....

She leaned across the stone windowsill of her sitting room, hoping to catch a glimpse of Nathan, the prophet, in the gardens below. He had become such a good friend since she had come to the palace to live, almost like a *saba,* a grandfather. She was hoping he might have a word of comfort for her.

Bathsheba knew she was pregnant again. She recognized the signs. Again, the child belonged to King David, but he was her husband now. He had comforted her in her grief at the death of their first son, and this new life was the result of his time with her.

She was afraid to admit how badly she wanted this child— afraid it, too, would die. Their firstborn had been the result of an adulterous moment, a betrayal of her kind and loving husband, Uriah. They had paid for it with the death of the child after they had grown to love it. She knew both she and the king deserved such a punishment.

A pang of doubt pierced her heart again. Were the whispers

true? Was David responsible for Uriah's death at Rabbah? Had he ordered the commander to place Uriah in a place of highest danger and then leave him alone to be killed by the archers of the Ammonites?

Bathsheba swallowed a sob. Uriah had been so good to her, and he had been such a brave and loyal soldier to the king. Could David have planned the death of such a man to cover his own sin, and then taken his wife? Surely the rumors were wrong. If they were true, she could not bear for David to touch her again.

She wished she could ask Nathan, the prophet, about Uriah's death. He must know. If David had not admitted it to him, *haShem* surely had told him. She would not ask, though. Maybe she really did not want to know.

There was Nathan, walking just beyond the lily pond in the shadows of the juniper trees. Bathsheba gathered her skirts and ran from the palace into the gardens.

"*Erev tov,* Bathsheba *yekarah,*" Nathan greeted her.

A shiver of pleasure passed through her at the old man's easy use of the term *dear.* "You will instruct my son, won't you, *Moreh?*" she blurted.

He smiled. "And what if this little one is a daughter, my lady?"

Bathsheba wasn't surprised that he knew she was with child again. "I ... I'm sure it is a son, *Saba.* And I want him to grow up surrounded by your wisdom ... *if* he grows up." A tear slid down her cheek.

"Ah, dear one, you must not be fearful," Nathan murmured, pulling her to him as a grandfather would comfort a sorrowing child. "You have repented and been forgiven of the sin. *Yahweh* is not angry with you. This little one will live, my lady, and, yes, it is a man child, a son to help fill the void of the little one so recently taken from you."

She stepped back to look into his eyes, afraid to hope. Even David had repented. Perhaps *Adonai* would allow this new little one to live. It had been so hard to watch the first one die.

Nathan gave her shoulders a slight shake. "Listen to me. This child will live, and he is merely the first of four. One of your sons will be the next to sit on the throne of Israel."

Bathsheba gasped. "But what about Absalom? Or if not he, then Adonijah? They are first in line, far ahead of any child I might have, and there are others."

"The Holy One of Israel has revealed it to me, Bathsheba," Nathan insisted, wiping the tear from her cheek with one dry, rough finger. "Your child will be king, and he will be the wisest king Israel has ever known."

Bathsheba shook her head in wonder. She never had known the old prophet to be mistaken. When he said *haShem,* the Name, had revealed it to him, surely it would come to pass.

"If he grows up under your tutelage, *Saba,* he will be wise. I want no one else to teach my sons," she repeated firmly.

The old man smiled and bowed slightly. "As it pleases the king," he agreed. "I will teach them all I know, Bathsheba *yekarah,*" he promised.

She hugged him, her heart full of joy. *Yahweh* was not angry with her. Her child would live.

We can only hope Bathsheba knew what we know: *Repentance + Confession = Forgiveness.* End of story. Or perhaps that's just the beginning....

2

THE PRODIGAL'S MOTHER

THEME: *Hope*

Scripture: Luke 15:11–32

*T*ikvah gave the mound of dough a hurried last knead, shaped it into a round loaf, and covered it with a cloth. Placing the loaf near the hearth to rise, she called to the servant girl, "The lamb will be ready for turning in a few minutes, Agar. I'm going out to find some flowers for the table, but I will be back before the bread is ready for the oven."

Feeling a twinge of guilt for the half lie, she took a thin shawl from the hook beside the back door and threw it over her head to protect it from the baking sun. *I will try to find some flowers*, she promised herself as she went into the garden, *if there are any that have not shriveled up in this terrible heat.* However, finding flowers to grace the table for the *arukhot erev,* the evening meal, was not her reason for wandering down the lane toward the main road.

Each day since their youngest son had eagerly grasped the purse filled with coins from his father's hand and gone off whistling toward some far country, her husband had climbed the highest hill at the edge of their lands and eagerly watched the road that wound into the distance. When he could delay the evening meal no longer, he would come trudging to the house, his head lowered, walking like a man twice his age.

She shaded her eyes with her hand. There he was, leaning forward a little as though to narrow the distance that stretched between him and his errant son.

Though Tikvah rarely left the stone walls of their home to walk to the highest hill and peer out toward whatever strange place held her son, the eyes of her heart watched for him all day, every day, and throughout the long nights of restless sleep.

She ached with yearning to smooth the black tangled curls from his forehead as she had done when he was a toddler, to see his dark eyes laughing up at her as he related his adventuresome day. She longed to hold him against her as he cried out from some nightmare or wept over some cruel remark from his older brother.

There had been no word from him these many months, except the tidbits of gossip she overheard as the servant girls whispered among themselves. He was spending his money quickly, becoming popular as he treated new, unsavory companions to feasting and riotous living.

Benjamin reported the other day that Saul's money was gone and he was reduced to feeding the swine of a prosperous farmer near the Tigris River. She had no idea where her older son got his information, but she hoped his report was exaggerated.

Her mind was filled with concern. *Does Saul have food to eat when his stomach growls with hunger? Does he have a warm bath and clean clothes when he comes in covered with filth from feeding the swine, a job no self-respecting Jew would take?*

She hoped the tale was spun from Benjamin's bitter satisfaction in seeing his rebellious brother receive what he felt was his due.

She had heard, though, that a great famine had struck the land where Saul had gone. Her husband had reported that the merchants who came to trade at the gates of the city spoke of little else than the merciless heat that had burned crops and dried wells and streams in the lands around them. "If the rains don't come soon," he had said, "our own land will suffer the same fate."

"*Yahweh* will send the rain in time, Aaron," she had comforted. "He always hears our prayers and answers just in time."

Aaron had smiled then, a small smile, half of what once had spread his generous mouth in pleasure. Aaron had not truly smiled since Saul had left.

"You are right, Tikvah," he had agreed. "The God of Israel hears the prayers of his people. What are the gods of those foreign places?" Aaron had spat upon the ground. "They are worthless idols, made by the hands of men and carried wherever they must go. They have no power to do anything. We must trust in *Yahweh.*"

Tikvah knew her husband was thinking again of their wandering son. They must keep strong the hope that *Yahweh* would bring him home.

Sometimes she wondered if they had been remiss in heeding

the warnings of the Proverbs that to "spare the rod is to spoil the child." She knew Aaron had tried to properly discipline both of their sons, to bring them up in the nurture and admonition of the Lord. She had supported all his efforts.

Beni had never needed more than a verbal correction, for he lived to please his father. From the beginning Saul was different. This mischievous younger son had been so easy to love and so hard to punish.

"Oh, *haShem,*" she prayed, "we tried. Forgive us if we did not punish him often enough or severely enough. Forgive us and him, and please keep him safe."

Her favorite psalm spread over her mind like a soothing balm. "Weeping may remain for a night, but rejoicing comes in the morning." She was convinced that, one day, her long night of weeping would be over and her child would come home. Her hope in *haShem* was alive and well.

Today, though, she felt more than hope fueling her prayers. She felt her youngest son had a great need that she could not meet because she did not know where he was. Was he hungry? Was he sick? Or, *Adonai* forbid! Was he …? She choked on the thought.

Oh, haShem, name of all names, please do not let him be dead in his sins. Whatever he has become, however he has strayed, please bring him home to me. I will feed him. I will nurture him back to health. I will coax him back to you. Just let him be alive. And bring him home!

She swallowed hard and dabbed with the hem of the shawl at the hot tears that spilled from her eyes.

"Going out like *Abba* to watch the road for that errant son of yours, *Imah?*"

"You startled me, Beni," she scolded, swiping furtively at the tears with her fingertips. "I thought I would try to find some flowers for the evening table, but it seems the sun has devoured them all."

"*Imah,* it is not like you to be dishonest," Benjamin's deep voice scolded back. "I know *Abba* stands each day in the fading sun, hoping against hope to see Saul coming down the road. Can't the two of you admit that your youngest son is a wastrel and an ingrate, and let him go?"

"Beni! He is your brother!"

"He is no true brother of mine, *Imah!* I tried to warn you and *Abba* that spoiling him rotten would lead to no good end, but you could deny him nothing. Now see what ..."

"Beni, Beni," she interrupted, "must you be so bitter? Your brother, whether or not you like to acknowledge him as that, is lost. He is lost to us and to God. Of course, your father longs for his return, as do I." She reached over to pat his broad shoulder, but he shrugged out of her reach.

She sighed. "You are a good son, Beni. You are hardworking and frugal. You are a wise and trustworthy manager of our lands and servants. You are faithful in attendance at synagogue. Your reading of the scrolls is the best in the congregation."

"You are my mother," Benjamin retorted wryly. "You are just a little prejudiced, I would venture."

"Only a little, Beni.

"I hope you know how much we appreciate you, Beni, how highly your father and I think of you."

He grunted. "You, perhaps, *Imah. Abba* thinks of nothing but his baby boy and if he will be home in time for the evening meal." He threw the mocking words over his shoulder as he turned and headed toward the stables.

Oh, my son, my son. Tikvah mourned, as concerned for the state of her oldest son as she was for her wandering prodigal. Benjamin always had been sober and steady, but he had grown bitter in these months since Saul had left him to carry on the work alone.

Not that Saul had been much help when he was there. It was Beni's frequent complaint that his brother dug in the soil only long enough to find fishing worms and then run off to the river to fish, that he set the dog to chasing the cows so that their milk soured and their calves bawled, that he tucked the fowl's heads under their wings and twirled them around until they staggered like drunkards when he set them down.

Mischievous Saul had been a trial at times. Benjamin always had been the dependable one, though sometimes she had wished he might be a little more like Saul and enjoy life just a little. He was so serious, so dedicated to work and profit and the growth of their holdings.

Aaron had been much like that when he was Beni's age, nearing thirty. He, too, had been a hard worker, trustworthy, honest, dedicated. Yet—praise be to *haShem*—he had mellowed. He had grown content with their home and their lands, with the two children with whom *Adonai* had seen fit to bless them.

She sighed. Saul's leaving had changed her husband beyond recognition. He had become an old man, his eyes faded from peering futilely into the sun, his joy in life shriveled from grief like the vegetation along the road had shriveled in the unrelenting heat of the sun. And she supposed Aaron had become oblivious to the fine traits of his elder son in his grief for his younger boy.

She often had been exasperated with her mischievous, laughing Saul. But he was her son, born when she had thought she would not be blessed with another child, and she loved him with all her heart—as she did Beni. Her heart ached for both of them.

Oh, haShem, help my eldest son to become more loving, and please, bring my baby home.

JOANNE

My friend, whom I will call Joanne, was awakened by the shrill sound of the telephone in the middle of the night.

"Hello?" she answered, knowing the call would be bad news, knowing it would be about Camille. *Oh, God,* she begged silently, unable to finish the prayer.

"Mrs. Ross?" a vaguely familiar voice asked.

"Yes," she answered, wanting to get it over and yet not wanting to hear.

"This is Doctor Aman at St. Luke's. We have your daughter here in ICU again."

"Is she …? Is she …?" Joanne swallowed the lump blocking her voice, cleared her throat, and started again. "How bad is she?" she finally managed.

"Well, she OD'd again this evening, Mrs. Ross. I'm sorry."

"Is she …? Will she …?" Joanne heard her voice rise in fear.

"It was close this time, but I … I think she will make it," the doctor said.

Joanne's heart stopped, then began again with a thump. She had picked up the hesitation in his voice. He wasn't sure Camille would live.

"May I speak with her?" she blurted.

"I'm afraid that's impossible right now," he said. "We have her on a ventilator. Perhaps you could call tomorrow."

A ventilator? The word struck terror in her heart. "I'll be there before then, doctor," she interrupted, already preparing her mind for the four-hour drive. "I'll be there," she repeated, hanging up the phone.

A sob clawed at her throat, but she swallowed it. *This is no time to give in to despair,* she cautioned herself, throwing essentials into a carryall. *I've got to get to Camille, to hold her in my arms, to assure her it will be all right.*

But would it? Would Camille ever be all right again? Joanne had such hopes that this new program would work, that her prayers finally would be answered, and her daughter would be freed from her addictions. Even in those times when she had heard Camille railing against God, begging him to leave her alone, to let her die, she had been sure God had promised not to let her go.

Suddenly, she wondered if that comforting thought had come from her own desperate longings. Had she deceived herself into thinking she'd heard God's promise? Was it already too late for Camille?

"'No one who puts his hand to the plow and looks back is fit for service in the kingdom of God,'" the pastor had quoted from Luke 9:62 in his sermon last Sunday.

Camille once had "put her hand to the plow," Joanne knew. She once had loved working in the church, and had trusted Jesus for everything from healing scraped knees to resurrecting her near-dead cat. What had driven her little girl so far from God? What had pushed her to the place where she might no longer be fit for the kingdom of God?

Oh, God! She grabbed her purse, the carryall, and her car keys and ran from the house.

She climbed behind the wheel of her small blue Nissan, backed into the street, and headed north, her foot pressing the accelerator just enough to keep below the excusable five miles above the speed limit.

As she drove, her mind replayed the years she had spent raising Camille. She was the baby, a delightful pixie child who ran through their lives on tiptoe, as though she must hurry to explore the world and everything in it. She supposed that was what had gotten her into drugs—that desire to experience everything.

Tears stung Joanne's eyes as she recalled precious years at home with Camille before she joined the others at school. It seemed no time at all since she was skipping through the house, playing some imaginative game.

Her favorite was *Hansel and Gretel.* "Mama, may I go outside and get some pebbles to mark the path so Gretel and I can find our way home through the forest?" she might ask. "Crumbs don't work, you know, 'cause the birds eat 'em."

Surely that delightful child is still there, buried under the debris of rebellion and sin. Surely that beautiful little girl could find her way home by following the spiritual truths that had been planted along the path of her growing-up years.

She brushed futilely at the tears blinding her eyes, then gave up and let them roll down her face. *Camille is lost. If she dies ...*

"Oh, God," she moaned. "In the name of Jesus ..." It was all she could muster, this broken litany of prayer, repeated over and over as she sped through the night, hoping against hope that she would find her precious daughter alive when she reached the end of the journey.

HANSEL AND GRETEL

In the familiar story so loved by little Camille, Hansel and Gretel were the children of a poor woodcutter who was cajoled by their hard-hearted stepmother into abandoning them when times grew lean.

Overhearing the plot, Hansel went out in the night and gathered white pebbles from the yard, which he dropped to mark their path as they were taken deep into the woods and left to make their own way or die. However, when the moon rose that night, it shone on the white pebbles and the children easily followed the trail back home.

The determined stepmother secretly planned a second abandonment, and this time, Hansel, having no warning, was unprepared. He had nothing with which to mark the path except some bread crumbs from their lunch. To the children's dismay, however, when they tried to follow the trail, they found that the birds had eaten all the crumbs. Having nothing to follow, the children were lost in the woods and fell into the clutches of a wicked witch who wanted to eat them. You know the rest of the story.

The moral of this story might be that we must ensure that our children grow up equipped with rock-solid trail markers from the Word of God. Then, even if they stray from the path and become lost in this godless world, they can find their way home by following these eternal truths. Solomon reinforces this principle when he writes in Proverbs 22:6: "Train a child in the way he should go, and when he is old he will not turn from it." The verse does not say he will not stray, but it promises he will come back to the right path someday.

UNDERSTANDING TIKVAH

In the Hebrew language *Tikvah* means "hope," which is why we have chosen this name for our hypothetical mother of the prodigal son. The name would be pronounced "Teekvah," since the vowel sound of *i* in Hebrew is "ee." Likewise, the word for "mama" or "mother" could be transliterated "Imah," or "eema," but would be pronounced "eemah."

Luke 15's account is all about the man of the story, the prodigal son's father. Maybe the mother had died before the son left home, or died of grief after his departure. Maybe she died at his birth, which would explain the small number of children in times when large families were the norm.

At some point, however, the prodigal son had a mother, and if she were still living at the time of our story, she surely grieved desperately over her wandering son.

Some astute mother has said that to have a child is to forever have your heart go walking around outside your body. It doesn't matter how old the child may be, or how many siblings he or she may have, that mother's heart is with that child wherever he goes or whatever she does for the rest of his or her life.

Tikvah must have been distressed over her older son, also, for she surely knew his unforgiving heart could not be pleasing to God. Psalm 133:1 says, "How good and pleasant it is when brothers live together in unity!"

Jesus put it more bluntly when he warned in Mark 11:25, "And when you stand praying, if you hold anything against anyone, forgive him, so that your Father in heaven may forgive you your sins."

In Mark 11:26, the King James Version adds this sobering thought, "But if ye do not forgive, neither will your Father which is in heaven forgive your trespasses."

"I TOLD YOU SO!"

When we were enduring our children's various teenage rebellions, I once thought it would give me pleasure to someday be able to say, "I told you so." But I found that watching a wayward son reap what he had sown, or seeing a precious daughter suffer her just reward, gave me no satisfaction at all.

Unlike the prodigal son's older brother, a mother gets no joy from seeing her child reap what he has sown. She suffers along with him, holds out her arms, and says, "Come, and I will help you pick up the pieces."

Isn't that just like God? We may refer to him as "our Father," and describe him in masculine terms, but God surely has a mother's heart. He accepts the fact that we have messed up his best intentions for our lives and holds out his hand. "Come, let's see what you and I can make of what's left." And he can take the most shattered individual, the one who not only has missed God's plan A, B, and C for his life, but even X, Y, and Z, and put it all back together into something beautiful. He *can* do this because he is God. He *will* do this because he loves us. Enough to die for us. Remember John 3:16?

PERSEVERING IN HOPE

In Jesus' story of the prodigal son, the father had hope of seeing his son coming up that road, or he wouldn't have been watching so faithfully for him that he saw him coming home "from afar off."

Typically, though, it is the mother who keeps watch, whose every thought is a prayer, who keeps that lamp burning in the window to welcome the prodigal home. It is the mother of the convicted killer who holds vigil outside the execution chamber, hoping against all odds that at the last moment word will come that her child has been spared.

Jesus taught us never to give up, to persevere to the end, as exemplified in the story he told in Luke 11:5–9:

> Suppose one of you has a friend, and he goes to him at midnight and says, "Friend, lend me three loaves of bread, because a friend of mine on a journey has come to me, and I have nothing to set before him."
>
> Then the one inside answers, "Don't bother me. The door is already locked, and my children are with me in bed. I can't get up and give you anything." I tell you, though he will not get up and give him the bread because he is his friend, yet because of the man's boldness he will get up and give him as much as he needs.

Jesus ended the story with the admonition, "Ask and it will be given to you; seek and you will find; knock and the door will be opened to you."

Again, in Luke 18:2–8, Jesus tells his disciples:

In a certain town there was a judge who neither
feared God nor cared about men. And there was a
widow in that town who kept coming to him with
the plea, "Grant me justice against my adversary."

For some time he refused. But finally he said to
himself, "Even though I don't fear God or care about
men, yet because this widow keeps bothering me, I
will see that she gets justice, so that she won't eventually wear me out with her coming!"

Jesus ended this parable with, "Will not God bring about
justice for his chosen ones, who cry out to him day and night?
Will he keep putting them off? I tell you, he will see that they
get justice, and quickly."

MY OWN PRODIGAL

I "cry out to him day and night" for my own prodigal son. That
precious child who once made me Popsicle-stick picture frames
holding his picture, signed with "love." That delightful little boy
who saw God in everything from clouds to wooly worms. That
almost-teenager who cried because he could not lead his friends to
peace in God. That rebellious young man who now wants to run
his own life without interference from God or me.

If he were younger, I could discipline him—put him in

time-out, administer a spanking, deny him privileges. But he is a young adult.

Well-meaning family and friends have advised me to exercise "tough love." This works in many cases. When my brother, as he put it, "broke the dinner plate" of his hedonistic son, it made a good Christian man out of him. When my friend put her rebellious daughter out of the house, she straightened up and became a model young woman.

I don't condemn such action. But I have prayed long and hard about what to do in our situation, and the only thing God has told me is, "Love him." My son is adopted, and there are circumstances that have embittered him, filled him with low self-esteem, confused him, made him feel unloved and unwanted. God knows he needs to feel loved.

When I stand listening to my adult child's angry tirades at me, at God, at life in general, do I hate him? Once my responsive anger has passed, do I want vengeance? No. I just want to take him in my arms and soothe his troubled soul back to peace in God, as I once soothed his troubled dreams back to peaceful sleep. I want to help him find his way out of darkness and confusion into a fulfilling life.

UNCONDITIONAL LOVE

While having to deal with a rebellious child is not something I would choose to do, this experience has taught me something precious about God: He loves me no matter how stupid I may act, how hedonistic I become, or how much I beg him to leave me alone.

The unconditional love I have found within me toward my errant son—and toward his sisters who rebelled in their teen years—has made me realize my heavenly Father is willing to take me in his arms and love me back to him no matter what I have done.

As for my son, I am convinced that someday he will follow those spiritual pebbles strewn throughout his young years and will come home to God, whether or not I live to see it.

Back to Tikvah

The familiar story Jesus told in Luke 15 ends with the prodigal coming home to the open arms of his father, the joy of the servants, the resentment of his older brother, and … no mention of his mother. There is a big gap in the story where the account of his mother's joyful welcome should have been. It is likely that she no longer was living, but if she was, perhaps the missing piece of the story might go something like this …

Tikvah knew Saul was coming long before she could see him. She heard Aaron's shout of joy and saw him begin to run down the road away from her.

She turned and slipped quietly back to the house. Tikvah knew Saul would need a bath and fresh clothing, but first she would set before him a bite of nourishing food to fill his empty stomach.

What has my son endured these months? she wondered, as she slipped the risen bread into the oven, calling orders to her servant girls. *What is the condition of his health?* Beni had eagerly shared the rumor that Saul had been reduced to feeding swine. *What kinds of vermin infest his body, his clothes?* She shuddered.

She could hear Aaron in the front entry now, yelling for the servants. "Quick! Bring the best robe and put it on him. Put a ring on his finger and sandals on his feet. Bring the fattened calf and kill it. Let's have a feast and celebrate! For this son of mine was dead and is alive again, he was lost and is found."

Then Saul was there, throwing his arms around her, sobbing into her ear his sorrow for the pain he had caused her, promising to make it up to her. Tikvah could say nothing, only hold him tightly to her and let the tears of joy run down her face.

She cast a final appraising glance around the kitchen and sighed with weary satisfaction. The dishes and utensils were cleaned and back in their proper places. The floor was swept and fresh reeds had been spread over it. All was in order for the preparation of the morning meal.

Out in the courtyard she could hear the sounds of musical instruments, the singing and the laughter as Saul was royally welcomed home.

"*Todah rabah, Elohim,*" she whispered. "Thank you very much for bringing my son home."

"What is the meaning of all this racket?" she heard Benjamin questioning one of the servants as he came in from the fields.

"Your brother has come home, master, and your father has killed the fattened calf because he has him back safe and sound," the servant replied.

Tikvah looked up with a smile to welcome Beni, but she heard him swear an unaccustomed oath and stomp out of the house.

"Come, join us, Beni," she heard Aaron urge. "Your brother has come home. Come help us celebrate."

Again, she heard Benjamin swear. "Look, *Abba,*" he shouted, "all these years I've been slaving for you and never disobeyed your orders. Yet you never gave me even a young goat so I could celebrate with my friends. But when this son of yours who has squandered your property with prostitutes comes home, you kill the fattened calf for him!"

"My son," she heard Aaron answer, "you are always with me, and everything I have is yours. But we had to celebrate and be glad, because this brother of yours was dead and is alive again; he was lost and is found."

Tikvah knew there was nothing she could add to the wisdom of Aaron's words. In a way she could sympathize with Beni's feelings of resentment. He had been an obedient and praiseworthy son. He had walked in righteousness all his life. But somewhere along the way, he had strayed from the path of love and stumbled over this bitter root of jealousy.

She knew Saul had done much wrong. But, as Aaron had said, he had been lost and now was found. How could they not rejoice?

She sighed. Beni would have to follow his own path back home. There was nothing she could do but love him and pray for him, as she had all these months for Saul.

That's what mothers do, pray without ceasing for God to save those wandering pieces of their hearts out there. Galatians 6:9 says, "Let us not become weary in doing good, for at the proper time we will reap a harvest if we do not give up." So long as there is breath in our bodies, Joanne and I, like Tikvah, will never give up imploring a merciful God to save our prodigals. So long as there is breath in their bodies, we will never give up believing that he will.

3

GOMER

THEME: *Mercy*

Scripture: Hosea 1–3

Gomer pushed away from the wall where she had been leaning, wrapped her ragged shawl around her, and staggered into the wet street.

If I can just make it to my room before I faint, I'll be all right, she told herself, pushing with all her remaining strength against the downpour of rain.

The spring rains. Back home the garden would be planted and ready to grow at the coaxing of the rain. She almost wished she were there, tending her herbs and vegetables, preparing a nourishing meal for her husband and children.

She stopped, her need for breath stronger than her need for

shelter, as the rain soaked her hair and inadequate clothing. Then she stumbled onward, almost colliding with a man coming toward her.

The man threw her a look of scorn and crossed the street. She laughed weakly, ending in a cough. *That would not have been your reaction to me in the past,* she thought. *You wouldn't have been able to get close to me quickly enough.*

She supposed the man thought she was drunk, here in the middle of the day. And well she might have been had she had the wherewithal to buy the wine. But the pockets of her ragged skirt were empty, except for the crust of bread she had snatched from the hungry jaws of a cat in the doorway of the baker's shop.

At last she reached the hovel at the end of the street where she had been staying since being dismissed from the temple. They had discovered her illness and did not want a sick woman there to frighten the patrons with the threat of the silent death.

Is that what is wrong with me? she wondered. *Have I been cursed with that scourge by one of the so-called gentlemen who came to visit the women at the shrine of the great goddess?* She would have been terrified at the thought, if she'd had the strength to care.

I have served you well, oh goddess, she thought. *Perhaps you will protect me now from the silent death.* Not that she had served among the temple prostitutes in worship or belief in the goddess. She had been there for the gifts the men had slipped her, above their temple fee, and for the sacred raisin cakes she loved.

Her empty stomach growled at the memory of the raisin cakes, then filled again with nausea. She didn't know when she had eaten last. Yesterday? The day before? Her foray for food today had yielded only that small crust of bread. She took it from her pocket and began to gnaw at it as she slowly made her way to the table in the center of the small, dim room.

She picked up the oil lamp. *Nearly empty. I'd best save what's left for when I really need it,* she decided, sinking down on the rumpled narrow bed along the back wall.

She knew she was running a fever. She felt like an oven had been lit inside her body, and her mouth was too dry to manage the bread crust, despite her ravenous hunger.

Is it not the silent death, but Hosea's curse that afflicts me? she wondered suddenly. She would never forget his words. "Rebuke your mother, rebuke her, for she is not my wife and I am not her husband," he had said to the wide-eyed children. "I will make her like a desert, turn her into a parched land, and slay her with thirst."

Is that not what this fever is doing to me now? Then she remembered what he had said next, for it had sent fear into her bones. "I will not show my love to her children, for they are the children of adultery. Their mother has been unfaithful and has conceived them in disgrace."

"Only Lo-Ammi," she had cried out. "Only him." It was no good to try to hide it. This third child had been born too quickly after he had brought her home that last time. Hosea knew.

He had taken her into his arms then, assuring her that his words were intended for Israel, from their God, who wanted them to know that he was aware of their turning from him to the gods of the Canaanites. She hadn't known what to believe, but Hosea had shown love to her children—all of them.

Weakness swept over her, and she fell back against the bed,

stirring up dust that made her cough and gasp for breath. The fetid air smelled of stale cooking and burnt fuel, though there was neither in the dingy room now. She hadn't been able to earn a shekel for several days. If her illness had been apparent to the temple leaders, it surely would be apparent to any customers she might solicit on the street.

She pushed herself up and reached for the small tin mirror that had been a gift from that businessman from Egypt. It was the only treasure she had held on to when she had begun to trade her possessions for food, oil, and a place to sleep. Gone were the sparkling jewels, the rich linens and silks, the belts and sandals, the hair ornaments and musky perfumes her lovers had given her. But she had kept the mirror as a necessary tool of her trade, for better days to come.

Gomer grimaced at the grotesque image that stared back at her from the shiny tin—the skin parched and stretched tightly across her cheek bones, the once-lustrous dark hair hanging limply around her shoulders, the dark eyes sunken and lit with fever.

"Not even you would want me now, my faithful Hosea," she whispered. "I certainly am no longer 'your beautiful Gomer.'"

She sighed and fell back onto the bed. She could almost wish Hosea would find her and take her home with him, though she knew she would be bored and restless within days.

It wasn't that Hosea was not good to her. She always was happy for a little while, playing with the children, arranging sweet-smelling flowers around the house, preparing tasty meals for her family, digging in her herb and vegetable beds.

Then the boredom, the smothering sameness of her days, would build, and she would begin to long for the musky perfumes of Egypt, the sensual touch of silk and fine linen against her skin, the glitter of jewels and trinkets. Soon she would not be able to resist the excitement of other places, other men, and she would plot and make her escape.

Hosea always had taken her back. He even had forgiven her when she ran away with the Assyrian captain and had borne her third child too soon after he had brought her back. He had named the baby boy Lo-Ammi. The name meant "not my people." Hosea said the name was a message from his god to the Israelites, telling them their worship of foreign gods had separated them from the one true God.

Gomer did not believe that for a moment. She was sure Hosea knew the child did not belong to him and had named him accordingly. What he didn't know was that the child likely did not belong to the Assyrian captain, either. She was sure he had been conceived during the time she had spent at the temple of the goddess.

How fervently Hosea preached against the Israelites' serving the false gods of the lands around Israel. *What would he think, what would he do if he knew the child he is raising was a result of his wife's service to one of those foreign gods?*

Little Lo-Ammi could belong to any one of the temple patrons I entertained, even one of the Israelite priests who visited the women at the temple under the cover of darkness.

Her lip curled at the thought of the self-righteous priests, so pious and condemning in the daylight of the very sins they, themselves, committed in the night. *And too stingy and self-important to give gifts, beyond the temple fee.* When all was said and done, they all served the great god Self, just like all the other men who sought her services. She would have spat on the ground at the thought of them, but her mouth was too dry to form the spittle.

Hosea had tried to tell her of the God of Israel, whom he served with all his heart. She had to admit that, unlike most of the priests she had met, Hosea was sincere in his religion. He truly loved and served his *Yahweh*.

She supposed she had *Yahweh*—whoever he was, *if* he was—to thank for Hosea's forgiveness of her many adulteries. He always claimed that *Yahweh* told him to take her back, as an example to the Israelites of *Yahweh's* willingness to forgive if they would only come back to him.

The children are much better off with him than they would be with their mother. She had no doubt that even Lo-Ammi would be well taken care of by her husband. And he doted on Jezreel, who was the image of Hosea, and Lo-Ruhamah, who looked exactly like Gomer had at her age.

She sighed again. Hosea was a good man, but she often wondered if he might be a little crazy, with his conviction that his god spoke to him, giving him messages for his people. He even thought this god had told him to marry her. She laughed weakly, then went into a spasm of coughing.

Suddenly, from outside, Gomer heard footsteps. She grabbed a pillow and pressed it over her mouth to stifle the coughing, terrified that one of the creditors who haunted her day and night had found her. She had thought none of them would know she was here in this hovel, but perhaps the landlord had realized who she was and told them where to find her.

Or perhaps it was the landlord himself, come to toss her into the street because she had not paid the rent, or to sell her into slavery for whatever he could get. Panic seized her.

Oh, Hosea, she begged silently, *no matter how bored I might be shut up in your neat little house and gardens, come rescue me. Take me home.*

The heavy footsteps drew nearer. She could hear the rattling of chains. The iron band of fear tightened around her chest. Desperately, she glanced around the room, but there was nowhere to hide, no one to come to her aid.

LORETTA

I had known the person I will call Loretta all my life, but I hadn't seen her for a while. She had moved away from our small town to the city, where she had become a successful career woman. Then, her self-centered lifestyle was interrupted by a summons to return to her childhood home where her mother lay dying. When we got together after the funeral, she told me this story.

Fighting tears, Loretta ran from the house before Mama could tell her good-bye forever, as she had her younger brother. She knew she was no more prepared to go where Mama was going than Frankie was. Mama knew it, too.

Crossing the yard, she removed her high-heeled pumps, and gingerly picked her way down the rocky wagon road toward the barn. She stopped at the wagon, threw her shoes onto its bed, placed her hands on either side, and hoisted herself backward onto the weathered frame.

Suddenly, in the heavy summer dusk, all the neighborhood children were there in memory. "You're *it!*" rang out. There was the loud "twang" as a heavy foot sent the empty soup can flying into the weeds and smothered giggles as they all scattered to hide.

She could feel her heart pounding as *it* stalked her through the barn to where she crouched, holding her breath. "I spy Loretta!" Her heart stopped. Then, just at that last moment before she flew from her hiding place to race for the sanctuary of the wagon, there would be the heavy twang as a savior's foot sent the can flying and *it* back to retrieve it.

Finally, they would see the fireflies come out and yellow lights go on in the houses. A voice would call, "Time to come in, children." And *it* would sing out, "Allie, allie, all in free," to let them know the game was over, and all those still out could come in without penalty.

Loretta swung her dangling legs, trying to imagine the game being played in the court outside her restored 1910 townhouse. She'd bet her baby blue Corvette there wasn't a child in Louisville who knew the game. Or, if they did, it probably now required a specially made $59.95 can for kicking. Nothing was free anymore. Everything had its inflated, extortionary price. *And, yet, we all continue to pay it,* she thought sadly, *exchanging our birthright for a mess of pottage.*

She had meant to spend more time with Mama, but she had been so busy with her work at the university, so involved with the arts and the artsy, so … so empty, she finished honestly. Unsatisfied with the shallow, empty lifestyle, and with the shallow, empty people who went with it. And, in the midst of the crowd, so ungodly lonely.

Ungodly? The word brought her up short. Without God. That was what Mama had said to Frank. "It tears my heart out to tell you good-bye, my precious Frankie. But you are without God, and I am going to be with him. I won't see you again."

Mama had turned to Noreen and Richard. "I'll be waiting for you," she had promised. Then Loretta had run from the house after Frankie, before Mama could tell her good-bye, too.

Loretta heard the screen door slam and looked toward the house. She could just make out Noreen's slightly plump figure, peering into the deepening twilight.

"Loretta? Mama wants you. You come on now, you hear?" Norrie's voice was shrill with impatience.

Loretta sat quietly, knowing her sister wouldn't venture outside the yard in the darkness, any more than she had when they were children. She always had hung around Mama, tattling on the rest of them. Finally, Noreen disappeared, and Loretta heard the screen door bang shut.

She pulled her stockinged feet up onto the rough frame of the wagon, encircled the knees of her black silk slacks with her arms, and rested her chin on them, listening to the crickets and the peepers around the pond pick up their interrupted songs. Beyond the barn, a mourning dove uttered its grieving cry; deep in the woods, another answered.

Do they cry for Mama's imminent death? Do they mourn for Frankie's lost soul? Or is it to my own wandering spirit that the doves cry out a warning?

"Sis?" The soft query startled her. She hadn't heard her brother's approach. "Are you all right?"

How like Richard, she thought, to be concerned for her, rather than irritated like Noreen. "I'm okay, Richard."

She felt the wagon move slightly under his weight as he sat beside her, then his strong left arm encircled her shoulders. She leaned against him, trying vainly to remember when someone had hugged her simply because he cared.

"Mama really does want to see you, Loretta. She hasn't much time left."

She nodded against his shoulder. "I know, Richard," she whispered, "but I can't bear to have Mama tell me what she told Frankie." Her voice caught on a sob, and she took a deep breath. "It's true, you know," she said. "Frankie and I are more alike than you've ever been willing to admit, Richard—rebellious, restless, unsatisfied."

"There is a God-shaped space in each of us, Loretta, that can't be filled by anything less," he said.

Empty space? Yes, I have that, all right.

They sat silently for a moment. Then he said, "You, Loretta, are not like our hedonistic Frank. Yes, you have been a prodigal. You have squandered your riches among the heathen. But, unlike Frankie, you are aware that you are a sinner. And you spend your days—and your restless nights, I'd guess—on an endless, bleeding guilt trip, when all you have to do is claim your forgiveness. No questions asked. The blood of Jesus covers all your sins."

She smiled faintly in the soft darkness that now blanketed them. "Allie, allie, all in free," she murmured.

"Exactly," he agreed. "No penalty for those who are 'out' if they will simply come on home."

"Thomas Wolfe says we can't go home again, Richard," she reminded him.

"But John 6:37 says, 'The one who comes to me I will certainly not cast out' [NASB]. God loves you, Loretta. It's not too late for you, and Mama would so love to hear you make that new commitment."

She brushed impatiently at the tears spilling down her cheeks again. "I've been so far away, for such a long time," she whispered doubtfully.

He slid off the wagon and reached for her hand. "Come on, sis," he urged. "Allie, allie, all in free."

Loretta looked toward the house where the warm yellow light glowed against the darkness. She picked up her shoes, slid to the rocky road beside her brother, and took his hand.

MR. MACGREGOR'S GARDEN

You remember Peter Rabbit who—unlike his obedient sisters Flopsy, Mopsy, and Cottontail—was always getting into mischief.

When Mama Rabbit cautioned him never to go near Mr. McGregor's garden, where was the first place he went? You got it.

It wasn't that Peter was hungry. Mama Rabbit fed them well. He was plump and healthy. But there was something fascinating about that garden. Those tempting vegetables just over that garden fence and the challenge of eluding Mr. McGregor's hoe were too much for Peter to resist. So he risked everything— even his life—to enjoy the pleasure of a moment in that forbidden place.

UNDERSTANDING GOMER

Unlike Bathsheba and Justine, who happened to be in the wrong place at the wrong time, Gomer, Loretta, and Peter Rabbit deliberately chose sin over a life of respectability. Perhaps you know someone like that. The better things are at home, the more they long for the thrill of decadence.

Why did Gomer keep choosing the life of a prostitute? Why did Loretta continue with her brittle, empty life? Why did Peter Rabbit keep crawling under that gate? Why did they risk all kinds of danger for the temporary pleasures of their wanton lifestyles?

Peter was simply a hedonist. He enjoyed the thrill of the chase and the forbidden taste of the vegetables. It was good for him that he finally learned that none of that was worth ending up in Mrs. McGregor's stew pot, or catching a nasty cold from hiding in a water can and having to swallow a dose of chamomile tea instead of partaking of Mama Rabbit's wonderful gooseberry pie.

Deep inside, women like Loretta and Gomer, while also hedonistic, often long for a better life, but are not willing to give up the so-called pleasures of sin to get it. They may feel guilty for the wrong they know they have committed, but guilt is a destructive emotion. It leads to low self-esteem, which leads to more sin, and a continuing attempt to punish oneself or to allow oneself to be punished.

Gomer, though afflicted with the bored housewife's yearning for excitement, may have felt worthless. She may have felt unworthy of a faithful love like Hosea's and deserving of punishment, even if it was self-inflicted.

SOMEBODY HAS TO PAY

I used to think my grandmother was either a liar or crazy when she announced, switch in hand, "This is going to hurt me more than it does you." *Baloney,* I thought. *I'm the one with whelps on my skinny legs. I'm the one screeching in pain.*

It took my becoming a mother and having to inflict much-needed punishment on my own children, to show me that

Grandmother was right. I knew that "to spare the rod is to spoil the child," but I hated having to spank those squirming little rascals. I even hated having to enforce time-outs on those tiny, tearful rebels.

Neither does our heavenly Father enjoy punishing us. In fact, most of our sufferings are not punishment for our sin, but simply a result of it. For example, my alcoholic uncle who repented and changed his lifestyle, but later died of cirrhosis of the liver, was not being punished by God for his sins. He had been forgiven. Nevertheless, he still was subject to the harvest of what he had sown into his body all those years.

The murderer on death row who sincerely repents and asks God for forgiveness is forgiven, but he still may have to submit to that lethal injection to pay for his crimes against society.

As my wise grandmother used to say, "If you play, you pay." However, when it comes to the final destination of our eternal souls, Jesus already has paid the price for our forgiveness.

The sinner often feels she does not deserve God's forgiveness, that a just God cannot love her after all she has done. But God has offered us something beyond justice. If Gomer could look forward to nothing more than justice, she was a goner. What Gomer—and Loretta and all the rest of us—needs is mercy. Ephesians 2:4–5 puts it this way: "Because of his great love for us, God, who is rich in mercy, made us alive with Christ even when we were dead in transgressions—it is by grace you have been saved."

THE LUKEWARM

Some don't sink quite so deep into sin as Gomer. They just live out shallow lives keeping up with neighbors, making sure their children get to soccer practice and dance lessons. They become wrapped up in careers and absorbed in social activities and entertainment. And they remain unconcerned about spiritual things. If the thought that there should be more to life ever rears its head, they drown it with a martini or smother it with another social obligation.

Maybe your neighbors are like that, neither cold nor hot toward God, but simply indifferent. Jesus had something to say about that in Revelation 3:15–16: "I know your deeds," he assured the church in Laodicea, "that you are neither cold nor hot. I wish you were either one or the other! So, because you are lukewarm—neither hot nor cold—I am about to spit you out of my mouth."

If that cup of coffee I am drinking is no longer hot, I will pour it out and get a fresh, hot cup. If the iced tea in my glass has become tepid, I will get rid of it. We don't savor food or drink that is nauseatingly lukewarm. So we should be able to understand Jesus' disgust when we respond to his love and mercy with an indifferent shrug and an arrogant, "So?"

I have no intention of being lukewarm toward my Creator and Savior. But, at times, I find myself drifting into a remote, disconnected, uninvolved existence, watching from the sidelines as my spiritual life slips by. That's when I have to get back into the Word, force myself to concentrate on him, find every reason to praise him, and give myself a good shake back into awareness of the awesomeness of God and his love for me.

BACK TO GOMER

Hosea 3:1 tells us the Lord told Hosea to show his love to his wife again, though she was an adulteress. "Love her as the Lord loves the Israelites, though they turn to other gods," he said. Hosea obeyed.

Gomer could stand on the auction block no longer. The heavy chains around her clanked as she sank to the ground.

"Get up, you!" the auctioneer hissed, cracking his whip warningly.

She knew he didn't want her value as a slave diminished by any obvious weakness, but she could not have risen if her life depended upon it. *Perhaps it does*, she thought, ducking her head to cover it the best she could with her bound hands. She flinched in anticipation of the whip's first cruel bite.

"Fifteen silver shekels," she heard a man's voice call out. She gasped in astonishment. It was a hefty price for an obviously sick, possibly dying, woman, one with no beauty left to entice a man and little strength to serve him.

Gomer looked up into the eyes of Hosea. Her heart pounded against her bony chest. Her husband was buying her back. But why? She had sinned against him, time and again. Could he possibly still love her, still want her back after all the pain she had caused him, and in this unlovely condition?

"Fifteen silver shekels and eight bushels of wheat," the auctioneer bargained.

"Done," Hosea answered without quibbling. "Now loose her."

As the chains dropped away, he gathered her up in his arms, wasted body, filthy rags, and all. "My beautiful Gomer," he murmured, as he carried her to his donkey cart and settled her among pillows and coverlets.

She kept her eyes tightly closed, but was unable to stop the tears seeping out beneath the lids. She felt him raising her chin with one finger.

"Look at me, Gomer," he commanded. "You do want to come home with me, don't you?"

Tears flooded her sunken eyes and poured down her wasted cheeks. "Yes. Oh, yes," she breathed, as she sank into unconsciousness.

Hosea took Gomer home ragged, filthy, and diseased, but he loved her too much to let her stay that way. Just as we do not clean up before we take a bath, God does not expect us to be clean when we come to him. You don't have to clean up that friend before you can lead her to the Lord. God loves each of us—you, me, Gomer, Loretta—as much when we come to him in our filthy rags as he will ever love us. However, he loves us too much to let us stay that way, and he has provided the all-powerful blood of Jesus to make us clean.

Through Hosea's suffering over his faithless wife, God made it clear to faithless Israel that to regain his love and blessing, all they had to do was repent and come back to him.

Of course, it is a given that repentance has to include a resolve not to keep repeating the sin. When Hosea rescued Gomer from the slave auction, he told her, "You are to live with me many days; you must not be a prostitute or be intimate with any man, and I will live with you" (Hosea 3:3).

Likewise, Jesus, speaking to the woman caught in adultery in John 8:11, said, "Go now and leave your life of sin."

Like the reformed alcoholic or drug addict, I will always be vulnerable to temptation. We all will. However, 1 Corinthians 10:13 says, "And God is faithful; he will not let you be tempted beyond what you can bear. But when you are tempted, he will also provide a way out so that you can stand up under it."

IT'S FREE, BUT IT ISN'T CHEAP

Just as Hosea purchased Gomer's freedom from slavery, Colossians 1:14 (see in particular the footnote in New International Version) reminds us that God has purchased our freedom with Jesus' blood and has forgiven all our sins. All we have to do is accept it. The procedure is simple. It goes something like this:

Lord, I confess I am a sinner in need of your mercy. "For all have sinned and fall short of the glory of God" (Rom. 3:23).

I believe you have provided that mercy by sending your Son, Jesus, to die on the cross in my place. "For God so loved the world that he gave his one and only Son, that whoever believes in him shall not perish but have eternal life" (John 3:16).

I accept Jesus as my Savior and my Lord. "If you confess with your mouth, 'Jesus is Lord,' and believe in your heart that God raised him from the dead, you will be saved" (Rom. 10:9).

In other words, it's "Allie, allie, all in free," for all of us who will come home.

4

HANNAH

THEME: *Commitment*

Scripture: 1 Samuel 1:1–28; 2:18–21

*H*annah sat on the bench beside the back door, watching Samuel dig in the dry soil of the garden. He was always building something—a city, a temple, a sheepfold to fill with rock sheep.

Samuel was a special child—intelligent, creative, gentle, obedient, eager to please his parents and *Yahweh*. Though he toddled after his older half-brothers, eager to be a part of their rowdy games, he was different from the unruly children of Peninnah, Elkanah's other wife.

Hannah looked up into the hill country of Ephraim in the distance, aware that *Yahweh*, the God of Israel, was out there somewhere, watching. Not only was he the God of Israel, but he was *Adonai,* her Lord, who was always watching, and listening. Had he not heard her prayer that night at the synagogue in Shiloh when she had prayed desperately for a son to take away the reproach of her childlessness?

Elkanah had been good to her, giving her twice the material blessings that he gave Peninnah, trying to take the place of the sons she did not have. There was no way, though, that he could understand how she felt. He had not known the mockery of Peninnah, the shame she had felt as she shopped in the markets of Ramah among the smug women with their many children flocking around them. Even though her name meant *grace, Yahweh* had not graced her life with the children she so desperately wanted to give her husband. Then she had gone to Shiloh, and her life had changed forever.

She would never forget that time in Shiloh. They had arrived in the city late in the afternoon, and the little place Elkanah usually rented for them was taken. By the time they found a place to stay, the sun was sinking, and she and Peninnah were hard pressed to get the evening meal together.

"I suppose our good husband has again blessed you with twice the allowance he has given me?" Peninnah had snapped, as she divided rations among her hungry, whining brood. "I am the one who has given him the precious children he wanted so badly, and you are the one he blesses. All I get is more children."

Hannah turned away to hide her hurt. "Your children are your blessing, Peninnah," she answered softly. She tried to smile at the children as she passed them the wooden bowl filled with bread, some of it made from her own rations.

"Yes, I know," Peninnah's tone was sarcastic. "And you have none. I suppose a double portion of material things is cold comfort to a woman with the curse of *Yahweh* on her womb."

Hannah had set down the empty bread bowl and fled. She knew she couldn't swallow a bite of food. All she wanted was to get somewhere alone where she could sob out her misery.

Elkanah, though, had followed her. "Hannah, why are you weeping? Why don't you eat?" he had asked with his usual kind consideration. "Don't I mean more to you than ten sons?"

She had wept in his arms and then let him lead her back inside where she managed to choke down enough food to satisfy her husband's concern. She was aware that he loved her, but she also knew he had taken this second wife to give him the children Hannah had been unable to provide.

I love Elkanah's children, she thought. *I truly do, no matter who their mother is. But I have not spent one happy day since the first one was born and Peninnah began to lord it over me.*

Hannah had not complained to Elkanah about Peninnah's mockery, but that night in Shiloh, she had felt that she could not endure one more minute of sharing her home with this woman.

When Elkanah had gone out to ensure that their livestock and supplies were secure, Hannah had slipped off to the tabernacle to pour out her heart to *Yahweh.*

Oblivious to the chief priest sitting near the doorway, she had begun to pray—her lips moving silently, as her body bent and swayed with the intensity of her prayer.

The priest had mistaken her agony of spirit and had accused her of being drunk. She smiled at the memory. When she had explained that she was seeking help from the God of Israel to meet the need of her heart, Eli had blessed her with the confirmation that *Yahweh* would honor her prayer.

She had gone home filled with happiness, knowing that such a word from the priest was equal to a prophecy. When the answer came, this precious toddler who frolicked in the garden before her, she named him Samuel, which meant "the Lord heard."

From his birth she had whispered into his ear the stories of the God of Israel and his great miracles: the parting of the Red Sea, the falling of the walls of Jericho, and the child's own birth.

Pain knifed through Hannah's heart as she remembered the vow she had made that night in Shiloh. "O *Adonai,*" she had prayed, "if you will only look upon your servant's misery and remember me, and not forget your servant but give her a son, then I will give him to the Lord for all the days of his life, and no razor will ever be used on his head."

I have kept the last part of the vow, she thought, gazing fondly on Samuel's uncut thick, dark curls. *Now it is time to honor the first and most important part.* She could delay no longer, for the annual pilgrimage to Shiloh was upon her.

She and Peninnah had done little else lately but prepare for the journey, packing clothes and bedding, food for the family, flour and wine to add to the bullocks Elkanah would choose for the sacrifice.

She had not gone to Shiloh since Samuel's birth, using the nursing child as an excuse to stay home. But she had promised the Lord that as soon as he was weaned, she would give the child to him. He had been weaned for several weeks now. She could not postpone it any longer.

Never had she considered going back on her vow. She had asked for a child; *Yahweh* had heard and answered; now she must complete her vow. The only way she could have been freed from it would have been if her husband had refused to let her honor it. Only then, according to the Law of Moses, would *Yahweh* have absolved her from it. But when she told Elkanah about her prayer and the vow she had made, her husband had said nothing, meaning he would support her in fulfilling her vow, even though it meant losing a son.

Not losing him, she thought desperately. *I cannot bear the thought of losing my little Samuel. I am giving him to Adonai. I know he will be safe and well-cared for by Eli and the other priests, taught there in the house of God to serve him. Someday he will be a great man of God, a leader of Israel.*

Perhaps I will be allowed to see him each year when we go up to Shiloh for the sacrifice, she thought wistfully, watching the little boy, absorbed in his project. "What are you making, Sami?" she asked, moving to where she could lay her hand lovingly on the sun sparkles in his raven hair, her heart contracting at the thought of the brevity of her remaining time with him.

"It's a fortress, of course, *Imah,*" Samuel answered, his tone revealing his amazement at her ignorance. He shifted impatiently from the restraint of her hand, eager to get on with his business, then smiled back at her to soften his rejection.

What will he think when I leave him with Eli? Will he feel I've abandoned him? Will he ever forgive me for not bringing him back to the only home he has ever known, to his beloved garden, to the rowdy half-brothers he adores despite their thoughtless cruelty?

Hannah swallowed the lump in her throat and blinked away tears. These few remaining days would have to last her a long time, and she didn't want to stain them with tears. She wanted to cram them with all the happy memories they would hold, though all she longed to do was clasp Samuel close to her and never let him go.

Forgive me, Adonai, for loving this child so. He is yours. I do not question it. I would have it no other way. Just forgive me my mother's pain at the parting. Help Samuel to understand. And please, Adonai, give me the strength to let him go.

MEGAN

I handed the baby to the girl I will call Megan and left the hospital room, pulling the door behind me. As I went about my duties, I couldn't know the girl's thoughts, but I could feel her pain as she sat in that rocking chair, clutching her baby, tears falling onto his pale blue blanket.

The adoption agency's representative was waiting in the next room. She only had a few more minutes to hold him. These precious moments would have to last her the rest of her life.

I could imagine her tightening her hold on the sleeping infant, this week-old child with downy fuzz on the top of his head and a dimple in his left cheek. This tiny part of herself that she had not dreamed would take such a hold on her heart in the short time she had spent with him. *He's such a little person, so unique and special,* she must have thought, touching his soft cheek lovingly with her little finger.

The adoption agency would not let her name the baby. The adoptive parents would do that. But, secretly, she called him Ray, after her father. She tried to shut out all memory of the baby's father.

Megan was fifteen when she fell in love with Brian. They would finish school, get married, and live happily ever after. She was committed to that dream, to Brian. She would do anything to please him.

Then it happened. She was pregnant. She was sure her parents would kill her—and Brian. She could not bear the thought of an abortion, of killing this little part of her love for Brian. Maybe they could just run away, get married, and bluff it out, she planned desperately.

Brian, though, was horrified. He told Megan he wasn't ready to get married, that his parents were counting on him to make good on his football scholarship at the university and make them proud of him. Having a wife and baby at seventeen was not part of the scenario. He refused to go along with her desperate plans. When she refused his offer to help pay for an abortion, he told her callously he was through with her and that this baby probably wasn't his anyway.

She was crushed by his insult. Brian was the only one. The baby had to be his, and he knew it. Devastated by Brian's easy desertion and the sudden collapse of her dreams, Megan let him go. She told her parents, endured the shame and reproach, and agreed to go with her mother to a pregnancy counseling center.

The counselor advised her to complete her pregnancy and, if

she didn't feel she could raise the baby, to give it up for adoption. There were many good people out there, she told Megan, who wanted a baby as desperately as she wanted to get rid of hers. While he was just a faceless, unknown embryo, that was what she had thought she wanted.

Now the time had come to let him go. She would not know who adopted him, would not know where he was. When his birthday came, she would not be able to give him his first teddy bear or watch him blow out that first candle on his cake. *He probably will dive into it with both hands and smear it all over his face, like my little brothers did,* she thought.

She would not know if his hair stayed that golden color as he grew, or if his eyes changed from baby blue to green or brown. She wouldn't be able to guide his first steps, or hear his first word. *Will it be* Mama?*And, if so, who will she be?* The tears increased as she realized her baby would never know her. The rules of the adoption agency required that, for the protection of the adoptive parents, all ties with the birth mother be severed completely.

"You will never know how much I love you, little Ray, and will for the rest of my life," she whispered. *He would never know how she would search for him on a crowded street, how she would seek some recognizable feature that would let her know that child clinging to his daddy's hand was this little one to whom she had given birth. He would never know how she would study that little boy eating with his mother at McDonald's to see if he could be little Ray.*

I knocked on the door and ushered in the agency representative, knowing we were ending the young mother's last moments with her child. I ached for her as the woman urged, "It's time to go,

Megan." There was a touch of impatience in her usually sympathetic voice. "I have a long drive ahead of me."

I could almost read Megan's thoughts as she clutched the baby to her. *I can't do this. No matter how much I did not want a baby, I cannot give up this precious child. He is mine. A part of me.*

The papers had been signed, though, the commitment made to let him have a better life than she could give him. Sob as she would, there was nothing she could do but hand him over, and suffer that empty ache inside her deepest being for the rest of her life.

CASEY JONES

Once upon a time, the train engineer was every small boy's hero, and the best of the old-time train engineers was the legendary John Luther Jones, called "Casey," because he came from the small Kentucky town of Cayce. He piloted the fastest of the passenger trains, the New Orleans Special, better known as the "Cannonball."

One April night in 1900, Casey pulled into Memphis, Tennessee, on time, and found that the engineer who was supposed to replace him was ill. Determined that the train would complete its schedule on time, Casey climbed back into the engine and headed south.

Back on schedule and almost there, he saw a disabled freight train blocking the track ahead. There was no way around it, and no time to get the passengers off the train. If he jumped to save his own life, the train would hit the freight at full speed, and the passengers and crew all would be killed. Casey knew their only chance was for him to apply the brakes and hold them with all his might.

Staying with the train to slow it down cost Casey his life, but he saved every one of his passengers and crew.

You may have heard the song written about how Casey Jones "rode the Cannonball straight to the Promised Land." You may have seen his monument in the Cayce schoolyard between Fulton and Hickman, Kentucky. You certainly never have seen a better example of the true meaning of commitment.

UNDERSTANDING HANNAH

Unlike the stories of Bathsheba and Tikvah, the story of Hannah is not about the man involved. Though her kind and loving husband plays his part, the story in 1 and 2 Samuel is Hannah's story.

Hannah lived in a society every bit as patriarchal as that of Bathsheba, with few rights for women. Her existence was dependent upon the whims of the men in her life. Like Bathsheba, Hannah had been blessed with a considerate, caring husband who wanted her to be happy. For some women that would be enough, but in Hannah's day, the woman's most fulfilling role was that of mother, and Hannah wanted to be one in the worst way.

According to the account in 1 Samuel, Hannah's inability to have children was not an accident. It was a deliberate act of God, perhaps because he wanted to produce through her a special and wise man who would become Israel's most famous judge. And he knew exactly when he wanted that child to make his entrance into the world.

To add fuel to the flames, Hannah's husband married a second wife to give him the children she had been unable to provide. As this second wife's attitude toward Hannah became increasingly condescending and hostile, Hannah had no recourse. In those days a man caught in such an unbearable situation could seek a divorce, but not so a woman. She had no avenue of escape from the miserable conditions of her daily life with Peninnah other than death. Or to have a son.

Instead of taking her desperate need to her husband or to the judge, as Bathsheba had taken hers to the king, Hannah went to the only one who could solve her problem. If the God of Israel, for some unknown reason, had closed her womb—cursed it, as Peninnah said—then Hannah knew he could open it. She took her plea straight to him.

WHAT KIND OF LOVE?

What kind of love would seek a child so desperately, and then be willing to give it back without enjoying the pleasures of rearing it to adulthood? More importantly, once that precious, longed-for child was in her arms, what kind of love, what kind of commitment would it take to be able to fulfill that vow?

That kind of love is akin to the love a mother has when she sacrifices her own needs for the comfort of her children. The love of a tired mother giving up sleep to rock her restless child. The love of a destitute mother denying her own hunger to make sure her child has enough to eat. The love of a grandmother giving up retirement to raise her grandchildren.

Yet it is more than that. It is the love that leads a mother to surrender her own desires, even her own life, to the needs of her children. It is the to-the-death commitment of a Casey Jones. It is a mother praying with tears, "Lord save my child, whatever it takes," and being willing to die for the answer, if necessary.

It is the sacrificial love of Hannah giving her precious son into the care of Almighty God, knowing there is no safer, better place for him to be. It is the faithful love of a Jochebed placing her three-month-old baby Moses in a reed boat in the river near the spot where Pharaoh's daughter comes to bathe. It is the desperate love of a young, unwed mother letting her child go so he can have a better life.

It is the love of God sacrificing his beloved Son to bring salvation to people who don't deserve it, knowing many of them will not even appreciate it.

PROMISES TO KEEP

To help understand the concept of sacrifice, consider the different commitment required from a chicken to provide an egg for her master's breakfast and a pig to provide the ham to go with it. For the chicken, it is a day's work. For the pig, it is a lifetime commitment. For Hannah, Jochebed, and Megan, it was the latter.

Often a commitment is easily made in the urgency of a moment, then difficult to keep, leaving the committer seeking a way out. Sometimes it is better not to make a vow at all, as in the story of Jephthah told in Judges 11.

Jephthah wanted to win a war for Israel so badly that he vowed to the Lord, "If you give the Ammonites into my hands, whatever comes out of the door of my house to meet me when I return in triumph from the Ammonites will be the Lord's, and I will sacrifice it as a burnt offering."

Possibly he pictured a dog or a lamb, or even one of the servants running out to greet him. Obviously, he never thought that when he returned victorious from the war, it would be his young daughter, his only child, who ran to meet him, dancing to the sound of the tambourines.

Judges 11:35 reads, "When he saw her, he tore his clothes and cried, 'Oh! My daughter! You have made me miserable and wretched, because I have made a vow to the Lord that I cannot break.'"

Agreeing with her father that he could not break a vow to God who had given him this mighty victory over the Ammonites, the girl asked for two months "to roam the hills and weep with my friends," then came home and surrendered to the fate her father had brought upon her by his rash vow.

"Moses said to the heads of the tribes of Israel: 'This is what the Lord commands: When a man makes a vow to the Lord or takes an oath to obligate himself by a pledge, he must not break his word but must do everything he said'" (Num. 30:1–2).

Jephthah did not have to make his hasty vow. God did not require it of him, but once he had made it, he was obligated to keep it.

MY FRIEND BOBBY

I learned the hard way that inaction sometimes can be as deadly as action, that a lack of commitment can be as disastrous as a broken vow.

My first memory of Bobby was from third grade when he sat behind me, his shy, crooked grin telling me he wanted to be friends.

He was not an outstanding student. He was never voted "most popular" or "most likely to succeed." He was just one of those nice, quiet kids who often get lost in the crowd. He was someone who was always around, but would not have been missed much if he hadn't been.

In high school the journalism teacher assigned Bobby to my page on the newspaper, and I soon realized Bobby was a good one to have on my team. I could depend on him. He was always there with the news, accurately reported, before the deadline. He was reliable, steady, a hard worker, a team player who expected no glory for himself.

Bobby grew up watching his long-suffering mother endure the abuse of his alcoholic father. He even experienced some of that abuse himself. He learned to persevere, to survive without complaint, and without any great expectations.

When his father insisted he quit school and get a full-time job six months before graduation, he wavered. He wanted to earn that prized diploma. He had taken to heart the senior advisor's warning that it would be harder to get a good job without it. But he wanted to please his father, to end the conflict between them.

His classmates were indignant and rallied to give him the moral support he needed. When twenty seniors marched across that small stage on graduation night, Bobby was there, proudly clutching his hard-won diploma.

A bout with his father's old nemesis—alcohol— left him struggling to make a living and destroyed a marriage for him. Again, however, he persevered. And though he held mostly menial jobs, he managed to provide a decent living for the new wife and stepchildren he introduced to me one night at the funeral home.

Bobby was always there for the funerals of former classmates' parents, siblings, spouses, or children. He was always there for his old friends, quietly expressing his sympathy by his gentle presence.

Then I read in the paper that he had died "following a long illness," a losing bout with cancer. I hadn't even known. He was always there. He wouldn't be now, though, not anymore.

It was hard to imagine a world without Bobby. My husband and our children and I would continue to live out our days, and Bobby's not being there would have no impact on them at all. Yet a world without Bobby would be less somehow, diminished by the loss of one special, quiet person—by one missing crooked grin.

Suddenly, I realized that, though I had known him most of my life, had even prayed for him on occasion, never once had I told Bobby about the love of God that sent his Son to die for my sins— and his. The thought hit me with such force that it took my breath and brought tears to my eyes. If Bobby's salvation depended on my friendship, he would be spending eternity in hell.

Eternity. The word rang through my mind with the knell of doom. Existence without end. Such a long, long time. And for one who went into it unprepared, eternal darkness and despair without hope.

Bobby would have done anything to help a friend. I was his friend, but I had let him leave this world without telling him God had provided an escape through the sacrifice of his Son, Jesus.

Bobby and I always had been able to talk to each other. It would have been so easy to share with him:

Everyone is a sinner. (Rom. 3:23—"All have sinned and fall short of the glory of God.")

All sinners will die. (Rom. 6:23—"The wages of sin is death.")

Sin's penalty has been paid. (1 John 1:7—"The blood of Jesus, his Son, cleanses us from all sin" [NLT].)

We can be saved by believing Jesus died for our sins and asking him to forgive us. (Rom. 10:9–10—"If you confess with your mouth, 'Jesus is Lord,' and believe in your heart that God raised him from the dead, you will be saved. For it is with your heart that you believe and are justified, and it is with your mouth that you confess and are saved.")

Why hadn't I cared enough to share that with Bobby? I grieved as I took my seat in the funeral parlor.

The preacher began to talk about Bobby, whom he said he hadn't known long. *I've known him practically all our lives,* I thought sadly. *I've known Jesus nearly as long. Yet I never thought to introduce Bobby to him. It was just that I didn't want to intrude into his private affairs. I didn't want to embarrass him,* I excused myself. Then I had to lay aside those lame excuses. I hadn't cared enough. Oh, I truly loved Bobby, but my commitment to our friendship had been shallow, worthless. I had let my friend go to hell.

Then, as the pastor talked about Bobby's last weeks on Earth, tears of relief streamed down my face. Because this pastor had cared enough to visit Bobby during his illness, because he had been committed to sharing Christ with him, my old friend was not in hell, but had gone home to our Father's house.

He will always be there, as he was on Earth, his quiet presence and gentle smile adding something special to the space around him, I thought gratefully, trying to stem the tears.

"When I say to a wicked man, 'You will surely die,' and you do not warn him or speak out to dissuade him from his evil ways in order to save his life, that wicked man will die for his sin, and I will hold you accountable for his blood" (Ezek. 3:18). Because I did not warn Bobby, if he had died in his sins, God would have held me accountable for his blood.

Back to Hannah

Hannah's commitment was rock-solid. Iron-clad. She never wavered, as the end of her story confirms. After Elkanah had slaughtered the bullock they had brought to Shiloh for the sacrifice, Hannah made a mother's ultimate sacrifice.

Hannah took Samuel by the hand and, with the dreadful courage of Abraham leading Isaac up the mountain, led him into the tabernacle.

She said to Eli, "I am the woman who stood here beside you praying to the Lord. I prayed for this child, and the Lord has granted me what I asked of him. So now I give him to the Lord. For his whole life he will be given over to the Lord."

Hannah kissed Samuel goodbye, handed his little bundle of clothing to Eli, along with an *ephah* of flour and a skin of wine, turned and never looked back.

Did her mother's heart ache? Did her throat swell with unshed tears? Did she hurry to get out of sight of Samuel's wide, wondering eyes? Did she sob uncontrollably most of the way back to the hill country of Ephraim? Of course she did.

Did the three sons and two daughters God gave her afterward fill the void left by the absence of her firstborn? Surely not. As any mother who has lost a child can attest, dozens of other children cannot fill the empty place of that one.

All year long, Hannah worked on a beautiful new robe for Samuel, hoping her estimate of his growth was accurate. Each stitch she made was embroidered with a tear and a fervent prayer for his well-being. All year, she waited with anticipation for the time when she could travel to Shiloh and present her growing child with this small token of her undying love. She waited for that brief visit when she could hold him close for a moment and hear him talk excitedly about his studies in the tabernacle and the new, complicated project in which he was involved, now that he had outgrown building structures in the dirt.

All through the next endless year, she would treasure the memory of Samuel's quick hug and the light in his dark eyes as he murmured his thanks for the robe. As she stitched next year's robe, she would feast on small tidbits of conversation she had brought away from last year's all-too-brief encounter with her son.

Yet Hannah's recorded song of praise to God after she left Samuel with Eli came from the depths of her soul and was full of joy. It began like this: "My heart rejoices in the Lord ... there is no rock like our God."

We would like to think Hannah lived to spend long, pleasant hours of fellowship with Samuel when he grew to manhood and became the greatest judge Israel ever knew. We would like to picture him in his regal robes, his hands stretched out to hold the skein of wool as she knitted, telling her eagerly about his plans to lead Israel in some new, exciting venture. (It could have happened.)

Tradition says Jochebed died before Moses came back from his forty years of exile in the desert to lead the Israelites to their Promised Land. Still we would like to think that he visited her in the years when he was rejecting his favored position in Pharaoh's palace and drawing closer to his Hebrew roots. We would like to imagine that, as they chatted over latkes and hot tea, Jochebed was able to glimpse the mighty man of God she had diligently taught him to be in his earliest years.

We would like to believe Megan was able to meet her baby boy years later, and that they developed a forgiving, loving relationship that filled in empty spaces for both of them.

I would like to think that when I meet up with Bobby on the streets of heaven he will forgive me. I know I can depend on Bobby. He's that kind of friend.

Still, I live with the haunting memory that if Bobby had only me to depend on, he would be spending eternity in hell. It makes me think seriously about commitment.

5

REBEKAH

THEME: *Patience*

Scripture: Genesis 27:1–46

*T*hrough the curtains of her husband's bedchamber, Rebekah heard Isaac's voice telling Esau to get his quiver and bow and go hunting for wild game. It wasn't all that unusual to hear the father ask his elder son for a wild meat dish. But what sent a chill through Rebekah was when she heard Isaac say to Esau, "I am an old man, now, and don't know how soon I'll die. Prepare the meat for me and bring it to me to eat so I may give you my blessing before I die," Isaac said.

Rebekah gasped. Isaac was determined to give the birthright blessing to Esau, despite the message from *Yahweh* before the twins were born: "Two nations are in your womb, and two peoples from within you will be separated," the Lord had said that day she had sought the reason for the terrible jostling within her womb. "One people will be stronger than the other, and the older will serve the younger."

If the older were to serve the younger, Esau would serve Jacob, who was born seconds after his twin, holding on to his heel, as though he would supplant him as firstborn.

From the beginning Jacob had proved himself superior to Esau. He walked first. He talked first. He excelled in his studies. As he grew, he absorbed everything he could learn from Isaac and the head herdsmen and shepherds as they worked with the herds and flocks.

Esau couldn't care less about the cattle, the sheep and goats, the camels. All he cared about was stalking wild game in the wilderness, or frolicking with the two ignorant Hittite women he had married.

How miserable our lives have been since Esau brought them here, Rebekah thought. Even Isaac could not bear to be in the same room with them. Couldn't he see the lack of discernment Esau had shown when he had married them?

If only Isaac could see how unfit for the role of patriarch his precious Esau was. Obviously, it was Jacob who should receive the blessing, who was the son capable of leading the family, of leading a nation, if what *Yahweh* had predicted came true. And she supposed it must, since it was spoken by the God of Israel himself.

Isaac, though, would not hear of it. "It is Esau's birthright," he had insisted. "I will give it to no other, Rebekah. *Yahweh* will work out whatever he meant by that confusing prophecy."

From the day of their birth, Isaac had doted on Esau, who was so like him with his sturdy little body and thick red hair, with his love of everything outdoors and his disdain for anything refined or elegant. At times she felt her husband cared nothing at all for Jacob.

Jacob had the dark hair and eyes, the slender build of her family. He was so like Laban in his younger years that Rebekah sometimes called him by her brother's name.

She had loved charming little Jacob from the beginning and had forced herself to love the uncouth Esau. Eventually, both the boy and his father repulsed her; more and more she spent her time and her love on Jacob.

Isaac had not been repulsive when she first had come with his servant, Eliezar, to be his bride, she recalled. She had been a mere child, in her early teens, and under her veil, she had blushed at the sight of this muscular, forty-year-old man striding toward her, the sun glinting in the red highlights of his thick, curly hair.

Isaac had shown her every courtesy and kindness, and their love had been strong and beautiful then. Even as the years went by and she had not produced a child, her husband had not taken another wife, as most men did. He had prayed, not for his need for a son, but for her need to be a mother, she remembered, a soft smile touching her lips. Then, after twenty years of childlessness, *Yahweh* had sent her twin sons.

Rebekah stepped back into the shadows as Esau left to complete the errand his father had assigned him. Then, knowing time was short, she called Jacob to her.

"Listen carefully and do what I tell you," she urged him. "Go out to the flock and bring me two young goats, so I can prepare food for your father just the way he likes it. Then take it to your father to eat, so that he may give you his blessing before he dies."

When Jacob hesitated, she reminded him, "You know your brother traded you his birthright for a bowl of pottage that day when he came in so hungry from hunting that he thought he was starving."

How like Esau to think he was literally starving, she thought scornfully, *and how like him to care so little for his most precious possession. The birthright blessing would give him at least a double portion of his father's holdings, as well as leadership of the family.*

As Jacob hurried off to the goat pen, she could hear Judith and Bashemath bickering inside the kitchen tent over whose turn it was to prepare the noon meal. *What did Esau see in either of them? As a child, I knew more about cooking than they will ever know. They know nothing about sewing and weaving. They cannot carry on a decent conversation in our language. They aren't even pretty.*

What a mess Isaac has created by allowing Esau to choose wives from among the refuse of Canaan. Why hadn't he sought a wife for his favorite son from among their own people, as his father, Abraham, had done when he sent Eliezar to find her for Isaac?

Unlike his brother, Jacob showed no interest in the crude women of the lands around them. "I want a wife like you, *Imah,*" he often told her, "but where will I find one in this forsaken place?"

"Don't fret, *Yacovi,* my Jacob," she always answered. "We will find you a suitable bride when the time comes." Now Jacob was nearly forty years old. He needed a wife, but she vowed she would find one worthy of him.

Suddenly, a new thought hit her. At Isaac's death, if Esau became the head of the clan, would she be forced to give up the tent she had been given when she became Isaac's bride? Would one of Esau's foul wives insist on having it?

Her great-aunt Sarah, Isaac's mother, was dead before Rebekah joined the family, but from the moment Isaac led her into that tent, she had sensed her elegance in the delicate fabrics, in the hint of fragrance that lingered among them.

Outside, the once-black tent had faded through the years of hot desert sun to a soft brown shade. It had been patched in places, but the fibers had hardened and stretched taut in the winter rains until it was as waterproof and snug as a cave.

That tent has become more than my bedchamber, she thought. *It is my place of refuge—from the summer heat, from the winter rains, from the constant bickering of Esau's wives.* She shuddered to think what one of Esau's coarse wives would do to her beloved tent.

She could not let Isaac give the birthright blessing to Esau. *I don't care how much he blesses Esau, once he has given the birthright blessing to Jacob. When it is given, it cannot be taken back.*

Rebekah went to the doorway and looked out. Beyond the cluster of dark tents, she could see Jacob coming toward her, carrying the freshly slaughtered goats.

She took the fresh meat and began to cut it into the waiting pot of boiling water.

"*Abba* will know I am not Esau, *Imah,*" Jacob said, a worried frown between his dark eyes as he watched her add garlic, lintels, and onions to the pot.

Ignoring his comment, Rebekah measured spices into the pot. "This is the last of the spices until the peddlers' caravan comes through again," she mused. "I hope it is soon. Without spices my food will be as tasteless as Judith's or …"

"*Imah,*" Jacob interrupted, "no matter how closely you make the goat meat resemble Esau's wild game, *Abba* will know it is not Esau holding the dish. Esau is hairy and my skin is smooth. Even our scents are different. His voice …"

"Hush, *Yacovi,*" Rebekah admonished him. "Your father is old and feeble. You will wear some of Esau's clothes to carry his scent. I will make a covering of some of this goat's hairy skin for you. When Isaac feels your hands and neck, as he does to identify people now that he's nearly blind, he will believe you are Esau."

"*Imah,* I don't like to deceive *Abba,*" Jacob said then. "I know he has always loved Esau and cared little for me, but he is my father. He is a wise and caring shepherd and herdsman, and I respect him. I don't like to lie to him. I may bring down a curse on myself, rather than a blessing."

"Jacob, if you love me, if you value what kind of life I will have once your father is gone, you won't leave me at the mercy of Esau and his despicable wives. Let the curse fall on me. Just do what I say. Once your father gives you his blessing, there will be nothing Esau can do about it. It is binding, forever."

"Whatever *Yahweh* wills," Isaac often said. But Rebekah was not content with that. *Yahweh* had promised that "the older shall serve the younger." She would do everything in her power to see that this was so.

WANDA

I was climbing the steep rock face of the cliff overhanging the creek below. Gasping for breath, struggling for a toehold in the sheer rock, seeking desperately for something to hold onto. I had reached the end of my resources. Unless ... I extended my arm as far as it would reach and grasped the slender trunk of a bush growing precariously out of the rock.

"I will make it," I vowed determinedly. "I will."

Just then the bush broke off at its root. The security it seemed to offer was a false security. Inside, it was rotten and hollow. With nothing left to hold me, I began to fall. There was nothing I could do. I resigned myself to the inevitable. I knew I would be smashed on the rocks below.

Suddenly, a power swept under me, bearing me up, easing me down like a feather drifting on a gentle breeze. I hit the rocks with a soft bounce. Something had carried me from the heights of the cliff to the depths of the creek bed, unhurt.

I awoke, breathless and sweating. *I have always heard that if you dream you are falling and you hit the ground, you will die from the shock. So much for old wives' tales.*

It was just a dream, I realized, relief flooding over me. Still, I knew what I had just experienced was more than the surfacing of some deep buried fear, more than some relic of my overactive imagination, more than the reaction to the spaghetti sauce I had eaten for supper. It was a message, a warning.

I don't normally have prophetic visions. "Lord, if you sent me this dream, please show me what it means," I prayed as I prepared to attend Sunday worship.

"Someone here is trying to do it all," the preacher said at the end of his sermon, having no idea of the dream he was explaining. "The abilities and worldly helps on which you are depending are hollow and will not hold the weight of the burdens you are trying to carry. You must give them to God. He will handle them for you. You simply cannot make it alone."

This was exactly what I had been trying to do. The burdens had mounted—heavy job responsibilities, raising a small child, and struggling to send two older children through college, the life-threatening illness of my father and the increasing senility of my grandmother. I was determined to handle all of it, to scheme and manipulate until it all came together, somehow.

"'Come to me, all you who are weary and burdened, and I will give you rest,'" the preacher read from Matthew 11:28. *How I long to just let go and fall into the arms of God like in my dream. No more need to struggle for nonexistent toeholds. No more need to grasp for rotten supports. Just let him carry all my burdens and give me rest.*

Suddenly, I felt the peace of God flow over me like the relief I had felt at waking from the dream. My circumstances had not changed, but I could feel the stress draining away. My encounter with God in a dream had shown me I did not need to help God work things out. I just needed to trust him, to wait on him.

MACBETH

William Shakespeare wrote the play, based loosely on an era of Scottish history. You know the story: Macbeth, a Scottish nobleman, was crossing the moors on his way home from a successful military campaign when he met three witches who prophesied that he would become king of Scotland, though there were others ahead of him in line for the throne.

When he related the witches' prophecy to Lady Macbeth, she became obsessed with the desire to become queen and urged her husband to help the prophecy come true.

The next time King Duncan spent the night as a guest in their castle, Lord and Lady Macbeth conspired to murder him in his bed. His two sons fled in terror, and were accused of the murder. Macbeth was crowned king.

The crown, though, did not rest easy on Macbeth's head. Because he had murdered Duncan in his sleep, Macbeth was unable to sleep. He wandered the castle halls, lamenting, "Ah, sleep that knits up the raveled sleeve of care." "Macbeth has murdered sleep." Soon, in his growing paranoia, he began to murder all around him who might pose a threat to his kingship.

Lady Macbeth, driven mad by the horror of these murders, sleep-walked the halls, scrubbing at her hands, declaring that all the waters of the sea could not cleanse them of the blood she had helped shed.

Lady Macbeth soon died in her madness, and her husband was slain on the battlefield by Macduff, extracting vengeance for Macbeth's murder of his wife and children. Duncan's son, Malcolm, took his rightful place on the throne.

Had Macbeth and his lady been content to wait for the prophecy to come true by natural means, would their reign have been a long and happy one? Would the prophecy have come true at all without their intervention?

Shakespeare's fanciful version doesn't tell us. All we know is that Lord and Lady Macbeth's manipulation of fate led only to disaster.

UNDERSTANDING REBEKAH

Rebekah, also, might have shown a little patience and waited for *Yahweh* to bring about the fulfillment of his prophecy that her older son would serve the younger. Since this prediction was not from the muttering of witches, but from the mouth of Almighty God, Rebekah could be assured it would come to pass.

As a young girl, Rebekah, granddaughter of Abraham's brother, Nahor, had been kind and thoughtful, as evidenced by her generous watering of Eliezar's camels when she met him at the well. Apparently, her opinions were respected by the men of her family. When Eliezar came with Isaac's offer of marriage, her father and her brother consulted her before giving their consent. As uncharacteristic as this was in this patriarchal era, it was Rebekah who made the decision to leave her home and travel to Canaan to marry a cousin she had never seen.

Through the years, as she and Isaac grew apart, no doubt she learned to manipulate her husband to gain what she wanted. Schemes and plots likely had become a way of life for her. If she wanted something, she set about making it happen.

WHAT IF?

If Rebekah had not hatched her desperate scheme to ensure that Jacob got the blessing, but had waited on God, how might this prophecy have been realized?

What if Isaac, somehow, became convinced that *Yahweh's* prophecy and Esau's lack of appreciation for the birthright made it right for him to give the blessing to his younger-by-seconds son?

What if Esau decided he did not want the confining responsibility of the birthright, after all, and turned it all over to Jacob so he could spend his carefree days roaming the wilderness with his bow?

What if Isaac, in his growing senility, mistakenly gave Jacob the blessing instead of Esau?

It was God's plan from the beginning for the Messiah to come from the line of Jacob. In his omniscience he knew Jacob would be the more intelligent of the twins, the more thoughtful, and eventually the more spiritual. He would be the more suitable ancestor for Jesus.

All Rebekah needed to do was submit to the will of God and wait on him to bring it to pass. In John 8:44, Jesus declared that the devil is a liar and the father of all lies. Rebekah put herself in dangerous company when she, like Macbeth, decided to take matters into her own hands.

WAITING ON GOD

The Scriptures are full of admonitions to wait on God.

> *They that wait upon the Lord shall renew their strength; they shall mount up with wings as eagles; they shall run, and not be weary; and they shall walk, and not faint.* (Isa. 40:31 KJV)

> *"The Lord is a God of justice. Blessed are all who wait for him!"* (Isa. 30:18)

*"Wait for the Lord; be strong and take heart
and wait for the Lord."* (Ps. 27:14)

*"I wait for the Lord, my soul waits, and in his
word I put my hope. My soul waits for the Lord
more than watchmen wait for the morning."*
(Ps. 130:5–6)

Throughout the history of God's dealing with man, waiting
has been an important element of the relationship. Abraham and
Sarah, like Hannah and Rebekah, had to wait for God to give them
a son (Gen. 15:4 and 21:1–2). The Israelites had to wait 430 years
for God to deliver them from Egypt (Ex. 12:40–41). They had to
wait forty years in the wilderness before God allowed them to enter
the Promised Land (Josh. 1–3). The apostles had to wait in
Jerusalem until God sent the Holy Spirit to empower them to go
into all the world and proclaim the good news (Acts 1:4–8 and
2:1–4).

America had to wait on God to become a nation in 1776. The
Jews had to wait on God for the nation of Israel to be reborn in
1948. Even the creation, according to Romans 8:19, "waits in eager
expectation for the sons of God to be revealed."

I have learned that more is involved in waiting on God than a
stoic resignation to let enough time pass until he accomplishes
something. This "waiting on God" is an expectation, a trusting
that he will fulfill a promise or meet a need when the time is
appropriate.

Yahweh had told Rebekah that Esau would serve Jacob. Perhaps she did not trust that he would fulfill that promise. For some reason she felt she must make it happen—in her way, on her timetable.

I'm afraid I'm too much like Rebekah. Most of us are, aren't we? We have become addicted to instant everything—fast-food restaurants, microwave meals, electronic communications, fast highways, and faster skyways. No more slow-cooked beans in a kettle over the fire. No more pony express or slow boats to China. In the same way, we want God's promise or his help, and we want it now.

AN ON-TIME GOD

I could save myself a lot of fretting if I could remember that God's reputation is built on keeping his word. He may not come through with an answer to my prayers when I think he should, but he will be there right on time. He probably won't be early, though. Did you ever notice that?

I once heard a preacher tell of how he had received a call from God to travel from his home in Texas and take the presidency of a small Christian college in Kentucky. The problem was, he didn't have the funds to make the move. He was sure of the calling, but his prayers for financial help went unanswered.

As the movers backed their van up to his front porch, the minister went to his mailbox for the last time. There he found an envelope containing an unexpected check from someone he didn't even know for exactly the amount needed, plus forty-two cents.

"I've always thought the movers made a forty-two-cent mistake in their bill," he laughed.

I'm not a patient person. Like Rebekah, I am not naturally good at waiting. But, with practice, I am getting better at it. I have learned to spend the time in reading his Word, in praising him, in simply appreciating the things he has made—everything from the beauties of nature to the incredible intricate genius of DNA.

Then, when I'm not even looking, I find God has met my need and the problem is solved. It works better if I just "let go and let God," as we used to sing in Sunday school.

An Encounter with God Is Not Enough

Sometimes I have envied the intimate friendship that men like Abraham and Moses enjoyed with God. Their stories show that we must have an encounter with our Creator beyond the simple act of faith that brings us salvation through our acceptance of Jesus as Savior. We must have a meeting with God that changes us, that brings us into a deeper relationship with him.

Before Abram could have his son of promise, he had an encounter with God and was changed to Abraham (Gen. 17:5). Before Jacob could have his ultimate blessing, he had an encounter with God and was changed to Israel (Gen. 32:28).

Moses encountered God at the burning bush and was changed from a keeper of sheep to a leader of people (Ex. 3—4). Before the people of Israel could enter the Promised Land, they had to be changed by many encounters with God in the wilderness. Isaiah had to be changed by the touch of the hot coal to his lips before he could speak for God. (Isa. 6:5–6).

BACK TO REBEKAH

Rebekah's problem was that, although she had an encounter with God, she was not changed by it. She grabbed the promise and ran with it. By massaging its fulfillment with her own hands, she blocked any assistance she might have had from God and turned a potential blessing into a nightmare.

Isaac was not blameless, either. He ignored God's word that Esau would serve his younger brother. He disregarded the fact that Esau had married two pagan women unfit to carry on the bloodline. Worst of all, he made no attempt to discover God's will in the matter.

As blinded as Isaac by her determination to gain the blessing for Jacob, Rebekah had not anticipated Esau's violent reaction to his brother's stealing his birthright. She hadn't thought he valued it much, anyway. After all, not so long ago, he had been willing to trade it for a bowl of stew.

Both Isaac and Rebekah lost sight of the reason for God's establishing a people from the line of Abraham, a generation before. He intended to bring about a godly and just people who would walk with him in faith and obedience, and through whom he could send the Messiah. All they had to do was trust him and submit to his will.

Sixty years earlier, Rebekah had trusted an unknown servant to lead her to an unknown land to marry an unknown man. Now trust was no longer a part of her nature. When she saw Esau storm out of Isaac's bedchamber, swearing to kill Jacob as soon as their father was dead, she was convinced that, once again, she had to act.

Rebekah hurried out of the tent in search of Jacob. When she found him hiding in the sheep fold, she said, "Flee at once to my brother Laban in Haran. Stay with him for a while until your brother's fury subsides. When your brother is no longer angry with you and forgets what you did to him, I'll send word for you to come back from there."

She went to the well and drew a fresh pitcher of water. Then she went back to Isaac's bedchamber, a cup of cold water in her hand. She sighed loudly, as she handed it to him. She watched as he drained the cup, and sighed again as she took it from him.

"Why are you downhearted, Rebekah," Isaac asked at last. "I cannot see your face, but I can hear your distress. What is wrong?"

"I am disgusted with living because of these Hittite women," she answered, sinking down beside him on the bed pallet. "If Jacob takes a wife from among the women of this land, my life will not be worth living."

"Send him to me," Isaac ordered. "I will see that he does no such thing."

Rebekah stepped to the edge of the tent and motioned for Jacob to come inside. She positioned herself outside the curtains to listen, as Isaac spoke to him.

Suddenly, Isaac's voice rose emphatically. "Don't choose a Canaanite wife," he ordered. "Go to Paddan Aram right now, to your grandfather Bethuel's household. Choose as your wife one of the daughters of Laban, your mother's brother."

Rebekah listened as Isaac blessed Jacob and sent him on his way. When he came out of his father's bedchamber, she hugged him, handed him a bundle for the journey, and bid him a hasty farewell. She could hear Esau calling to his wives from the field, demanding a pot of hot water for his most recent kill.

Rebekah swallowed hard and brushed threatening tears from her eyes, as she watched Jacob hurry across the fields toward the north, the opposite direction of Esau's approach.

I will miss him so, she thought. *But it is necessary that he go for now,* she comforted herself. *Someday, when he returns to me, with a wife from our own people, I will again hold him in my arms, and perhaps his children as well."*

What Rebekah could not know was that in sending Jacob away from her for what she thought was a brief time, she set in motion events that would keep him in northern Syria for twenty years. In fact, Rebekah never would see her favorite son again. Her scheming had separated her forever from the only thing in life she truly loved. She would be dead and resting in the burial cave of Machpelah beside Abraham and Sarah long before Jacob returned to Canaan, bringing his wives and children with him.

Despite all her schemes, deceptions, and manipulations—or because of them—Rebekah spent her last lonely years in the miserable company of Esau and his wives, grieving the son she loved, longing for his return.

The end of her story might have been different had Rebekah waited on the Lord instead of turning to lies and deceit to fulfill his prophecy. In fact, had she not taught her favorite son to lie and cheat, he might not have been cheated, in turn, by Laban in his employment and marriage arrangements. Then he might have come home years sooner. In her clever plotting, Rebekah cheated herself out of the loving companionship of her son and grandchildren.

Jacob later had that encounter with God that changed him from a conniving manipulator into a patriarch, but, as Galatians 6:7 puts it: "Do not be deceived: God cannot be mocked. A man reaps what he sows."

Jacob reaped the consequences of his earlier deceit by being deceived, not only by Laban, but by ten of his own sons. He spent his later years grieving because he believed their lie that his favorite son, Joseph, had been killed by wild animals.

"A man reaps what he sows." As Rebekah found out to her regret, so does a woman. I don't want to forget that.

ABIGAIL

THEME: *Courage*

Scripture: 1 Samuel 25:14–42; 2 Samuel 3:3

*M*istress, you must do something quickly!" the servant cried, gasping for breath as he bowed before her. "The outlaw David and hundreds of his men are descending upon us!"

"What has Nabal done?" Abigail asked, stopping her packing of loaves of fresh bread into baskets to take to the shearing festival. "David's men have protected our sheep and shepherds from robbers all this time. What has turned them against us?"

"David knew it was the shearing festival," the servant answered. "He sent some of his men to greet the master and ask for some provisions. It is only fair, since they have been so good to us. But the master cursed them and sent them away empty-handed."

Nabal has put us all in jeopardy through his foolishness. But what can I do? Yahweh, *God of Israel, help me.*

"You know how the master is, mistress—no one can talk to him—so I ran to tell you that David is very angry. He and his men are wearing swords. They mean to slaughter all of us."

"Quickly!" Abigail ordered. "Help me load some of these things on the donkeys. Instead of taking them to the feast Nabal is planning, we will take these provisions to David. I only pray to *Yahweh* we are not too late."

As the servants loaded the donkeys, Abigail counted: Two hundred loaves of bread, two skins of wine, five dressed sheep, five *seahs* of roasted grain, a hundred cakes of raisins, two hundred cakes of pressed figs. She prayed it would be enough.

"Go on ahead," she told the servants as she mounted the last donkey. "I will follow." She didn't even consider informing her husband of what she was about to do. It was he who had put them in this desperate position.

David's deeds were legendary, from his triumph over the Philistine giant, Goliath, to his exploits in battle. Sometimes she watched from a distance as he competed with his men in war games, the sun glinting in the reddish highlights of his dark hair. What a valiant warrior he was. How proud his father and mother must be of him.

She had wanted a son in the early years of her marriage. Now she was glad *Yahweh* had not seen fit to give her children by Nabal. *I could not bear to raise a son like him,* she thought.

Since the day her father had announced that he had arranged a marriage for her with a wealthy sheep rancher, she had been faithful to that bargain. She would continue to honor it.

She sighed. *Living with Nabal has not been easy,* she thought. *The passing years have just made him increasingly churlish, loud-mouthed, and mean-spirited, and every year he seems to wallow more in drunkenness.*

She had come to despise the man, but she knew how to handle him, and she supposed she owed him something for providing for her so handsomely through the years. She prayed that she would be able to make amends for him, for all of them, with the man she was going to meet. It wasn't just a matter of saving face, as it had been so often. This time their lives depended upon it.

As Abigail rode her donkey into a mountain ravine, she saw David and his men descending toward her, all bearing swords. *Oh, Yahweh, help me to gain his favor,* she prayed silently as she leapt from the donkey and ran to fall at David's feet.

"My lord, please hear what your servant has to say," she cried. "Pay no attention to that wicked Nabal. His name means 'fool,' and so he is! But as for me, your servant, I did not see the men you sent."

David was looking at her, anger sparking in his eyes, but he had not raised his sword. He was listening.

"Now since the Lord has kept you from avenging yourself with your own hands, may all your enemies be like Nabal," she continued. "And let this gift, which your servant has brought, be given to the men who follow you."

David still said nothing. His keen eyes assessed the provisions she had brought, then came back to bore into hers.

"Please forgive me, master, for the Lord will certainly make a lasting dynasty for you, because you fight the Lord's battles,"

Abigail pleaded, and launched into a spate of words about how the Lord would preserve David's life and destroy his enemies.

She didn't know where the words were coming from, perhaps from *Yahweh* himself, but they poured out of her like water from a rainspout. And David still was listening.

"When the Lord has done for my master every good thing he has promised concerning him and has appointed him leader over Israel, my master will not have on his conscience the staggering burden of needless bloodshed or of having avenged himself. And when the Lord has brought my master success, remember your servant."

She stopped, breathless and out of words at last. David was coming toward her. He took her hands in his.

"Praise be to the Lord, the God of Israel, who has sent you today to meet me," he said fervently. "As surely as the Lord, the God of Israel, lives, who has kept me from harming you, if you had not come quickly to meet me, not one male belonging to Nabal would have been left alive by daybreak."

Then David ordered his men to accept her offerings. "Go home in peace," he assured her. "I have heard your words and granted your request."

Abigail was glad she had a donkey to ride back home, for her knees were so weak that she doubted she could have walked. *Where did I get the courage to speak so to this mighty warrior? He might have struck me down with a blow from that wicked-looking sword, taken the provisions, and gone on with his plans to kill us all.* Yet he had not. Surely it was all due to the protection of *Yahweh,* the God of Israel, who had sent her on this errand of mercy this day.

As she rode into the shearing camp and dismounted, the sounds of music and laughter greeted her. Obviously, the shearing was over and the feasting was under way. There was no sign of Nabal, so she left the camp and walked toward the house, leading her donkey. She could hear merriment from inside the house and found Nabal slouched at the head of the long banquet table, his eyes already glazed, his speech slurred as he yelled for a servant to bring him more wine.

Disgust rose in her throat like bile. She knew it would be futile to try to tell him now about their narrow escape from being slaughtered like the sheep they had roasted for this feast.

Thanks be to Yahweh *for blessing my efforts once again. But how tired I am of being the head of this household while my husband plays the fool.*

When he was sober, Nabal was a shrewd manager, she reminded herself, and had become wealthy, with thousands of sheep in his folds. He had built a fine house and filled it with fine furnishings. He had many servants to do their bidding. Abigail, herself, had five serving maids. But, even at the best of times, he was not a pleasant man.

She watched him trying to grab one of the serving girls as she poured his wine. Before long he would pass out and the servants would carry him to his bed.

Suddenly, she wondered how it might have been had it been David sitting there at the head of their banquet table. *Those thoughts are as foolish as Nabal himself,* she scolded. Anyway, she had heard that David also had an eye for the girls. *A man is a man,* she thought scornfully, making her way down the hall to the back of the house, knowing she was too exhausted to take part in the feasting, the merriment.

In her bedchamber she looked with satisfaction at the purples and blues of her newest silks and embroidered linens. Nabal had been generous in his allowance to her, she had to admit, but the material possessions could not compensate for the hardness of his heart.

Nevertheless, you are married to the man. You will grow old managing his household, smoothing over his mistakes, placating those he has offended with his foolish words.

Suddenly, the years stretched before her, month after month, week after week, day after day of doing everything in her power to please a man who could not be pleased. No matter what she did, there was always that sneer on his lips and that mocking coldness in his eyes.

If there was no Nabal ... But there is a Nabal, and you will belong to him until one of you dies. Oh, Yahweh, help me to bear it.

ELLEN

They had been good neighbors—this couple I will call Ron and Ellen—ever since they had moved next door six years earlier with their two daughters, Allison and Malinda. Since then, Katie, then Caleb, had joined the family and become a part of my life, as well.

In the evenings after work or on weekends, I would see Ron on the lawn mower cutting the grass around their neat Cape Cod–style cottage, or making some small repair. Sometimes he would drive off with Malinda in the car, I assumed taking her to soccer practice or a game. On Saturdays when the weather was good, I would see him throw his golf clubs in the trunk and drive off.

Ellen rarely took time for herself. She was one of those stay-at-home moms who rarely get a chance to stay home—always on the go to some school or church event, to the grocery or the mall; carting the children to a play, a concert, or the ballet—exposing them to culture and enjoyment.

On days when I baked, I would take over cookies or an extra loaf of whatever I had made, and we would sample them with a cup of tea. That's how it happened that I was there the day the school bus stopped out front and five-year-old Katie came crashing through the front door and ran straight upstairs to her room, dragging her well-worn stuffed monkey by one arm.

"Katie?" Ellen called, puzzled that the little girl had not come straight to the kitchen for her usual after-school snack.

"Mom, I need an old shirt for art class tomorrow," Allison announced, passing up my fresh-baked cookies and taking carrot sticks and a bottle of water from the refrigerator.

"Mom, Caleb spilled his milk," Malinda called from the living room.

"He's not supposed to take his milk into the living room," Ellen said wearily, then added to me, "but it's almost impossible to discipline a three-year-old when his father thinks he can do no wrong."

Before I could answer, the phone rang. Allison answered, then handed the cordless phone to Ellen. "It's Mrs. Jenkins, Mom. She says it's important."

Ellen took the phone. "Hello? How are you Mrs. Jenkins?" As she talked, she turned off the burner under the whistling tea kettle and poured the boiling water into a waiting teapot.

"Katie?" she said then in an astonished voice. "What did she do?"

Ellen listened, then promised, "Of course, Mrs. Jenkins. I'll be there."

She turned off the phone, sat two mugs on the table, and called, "Katie, come down here."

"I cleaned up Caleb's milk, Mom," Malinda said, throwing a wad of wet paper towels in the trash. "Can we have some cookies?"

"Thank you, Lindy, and yes, you may," Ellen said pouring hot tea into our mugs and sinking into the chair across from me.

"I can't believe Katie's being defiant. She's so easy-going, and she loves her pretty little kindergarten teacher. But Mrs. Jenkins wants to meet with me tomorrow after school. It must be serious."

"Will Ron go with you?" I asked, surprised she hadn't checked with her husband to see if his schedule would allow him to go.

Ellen shook her head. "He'll just tell me to take care of it. Katie, I'm counting," she called again. "One. Two ..."

Katie appeared in the kitchen doorway, her blue eyes flooded with tears. "I'm sorry, Mommy," she cried, throwing herself into Ellen's lap.

Ellen put her arms around the little girl. "What did you do, honey, to get Mrs. Jenkins so upset with you?"

Katie shook her tousled curls. "I don't know, Mommy," she sobbed. "Mrs. Jenkins told us to bring something for Show and Tell, and I took Spunky Monkey. But when I started talking about him, she got mad and told me to sit down."

"What did you tell the class about Spunky?" Ellen asked.

"I told them what you said, Mommy, that God made monkeys and God made people, but he didn't make people out of monkeys, 'cause if he had, there wouldn't be any monkeys left."

Ellen threw me a rueful glance. "Katie," she said firmly, hugging the little girl to her, "you did not do anything wrong. You told the story very well. I am proud of you."

Katie leaned back so she could look into her mother's eyes. "But, Mommy, Mrs. Jenkins is so mad at me. And she's mad at Spunky. She told me never to bring him back to school again."

"Well, that's all right, darling. You can teach Spunky at home. Now have some cookies and go play in your room while I visit with our neighbor."

"I wish now I'd taught her at home," Ellen said to me after the little girl had grabbed a fistful of cookies and run back upstairs.

"I wanted to homeschool all of them," she explained, "but when Allison was ready to start school, I mentioned homeschooling or sending her to the Christian school, and Ron threw a fit. He said he wasn't going to pay taxes to support public education and then pay again to send his kids to private school, and he wasn't going to waste it by having me teach them at home, either."

"My children went to the public schools," I pointed out, "and they turned out okay. There were times when I had to counter some of the science teacher's beliefs, but, all in all, they got a good education."

She reached over and patted my hand. "I know. I wasn't meaning to be elitist. It was just that I felt homeschooling was a good option for us; but not wanting to fight over it, I gave in." Then she shared with me the rest of the story.

Katie had come home from school talking excitedly about monkeys turning into people, and brandishing a book that neatly explained it all, leaving God out of the equation, of course. *If there is no Creator, there is no accountability to him,* Ellen had thought.

She had shown the book to Ron, but he had said, "Let it go, Ellen. Maybe God did it all through evolution. It doesn't matter how he did it."

"Ron," she had argued, "if we can't trust the creation story in Genesis, how can we trust the rest of the Bible? Do we just pick and choose what we want to believe?"

"Ellen, we can believe anything we want, but Katie has to get along in the real world," he had said. "Just tell her to agree with her teacher at school, and make sure she knows the truth at home." He was through with the conversation, already refocusing on the TV screen.

Ellen realized she had known for a long time that Ron's religious convictions only lasted until they began to embarrass or inconvenience him.

That night she had made sure Katie understood the story in Genesis 1: Man had not evolved, but had been made by God in his own image. She had told Katie that if God had made man out of monkeys, then monkeys would have ceased to exist.

"Now what do I say to Mrs. Jenkins?" she asked me. "Do I take on the whole public school system? Obviously, Ron isn't going to help me."

"Once, my oldest two daughters came home from school upset because their science teacher insisted they answer a test question with a statement to the effect that human beings evolved over billions of years from a one-celled creature in the ocean," I recalled. "She told them they would get an F for any other answer. My straight-A students were horrified at the thought. Yet they were old enough to know they believed in intelligent design, and they didn't want to lie about it."

"What did you tell them to do?" Ellen asked, hanging on my words.

I laughed. "I advised something close to what Ron said," I admitted. "I told my daughters to write, 'The textbook says human beings evolved ...' or 'The theory of evolution is ...' That way, they weren't saying it was true, they were just quoting what the book or teacher said."

Ellen chuckled. "I guess you were following the advice Jesus gave his disciples when he told them to be 'wise as serpents and harmless as doves,'" she said. "What happened?"

"They did what I suggested, and we never heard any more about it."

Ellen sat deep in thought for a few minutes. "I guess Ron wasn't as far off as I thought," she mused. "I still don't agree with his reasoning, but I know I shouldn't be so critical of him. He does have his good points. He's a good provider. He agreed to let me be a stay-at-home mom until Caleb is in school. He will gladly give Allison one of his shirts for art class. He will take

Malinda to soccer practice. He will buy more milk if Caleb spills it all."

I could see, though, that the well-worn mantra of Ron's generous qualities and love for his children wasn't working to overcome her resentments. Suddenly, she burst into tears. "I'm so tired of hearing the preachers preach about how women should submit to their husbands—how 'God is the head of the husband, and the husband is the head of the wife'" (see Eph. 5:22–23). At a loss for words I put my arm around her and let her cry.

"If I had a husband who truly knew God, who accepted his rightful role as spiritual head of our household, I would be glad to submit to him," she said, wiping her eyes on her napkin. "But I have to fight to get him to attend church services, and make excuses for him when he doesn't show up. I have to sneak donations out of the grocery money because he refuses to tithe."

She stopped and took a deep breath. "I know I shouldn't be talking like this," she said, "but if I submitted entirely to my husband, we would go to church on Easter and Christmas. We would toss a dollar into the collection plate on those occasions, and go about our lives free of Ron's dreaded embarrassments or inconveniences brought on by trying to have a relationship with God."

I knew the old admonition not to be unequally yoked with unbelievers did not apply to Ellen. She had told me some time ago that she had refused to marry Ron until she knew he had accepted Christ as his Savior and been baptized. She had been convinced that would ensure them of a happy marriage with God at its center. *Just another little girl believing in fairy tales,* I thought.

Impatiently, she brushed tears away. "I don't want to be the spiritual head of this household," she said bitterly, "but somebody has to bring up these children in the 'fear and admonition of the Lord,' and it looks like I'm elected."

I prayed with her and got up to go. "Jesus, please help me," I heard her whisper, as I headed home.

UNDERSTANDING ABIGAIL

Beautiful Abigail found herself, through no fault of her own, in the miserable situation Ellen and many other women find themselves in today. She had to be the head of her household because the man she married refused to accept the responsibility.

Oh, Nabal made a good living. He was a shrewd sheep rancher and prospered greatly. He filled their house with luxuries. He dressed her in silks, fine linens, and jewels. He provided servants to keep the household and the business running smoothly.

Perhaps, sometimes, he accompanied his wife to a wedding or *bar mitzvah*. After all, the wine would flow. Sometimes he may even have gone with her to tabernacle. After all, it was good for business. For the most part, however, he left the social and spiritual responsibilities to Abigail, spending his days bullying everyone around him and his nights in a drunken stupor.

Abigail had married him, though. Most likely her father had arranged the marriage, but Abigail knew she was stuck with it until the death of one of them severed the union. Nabal appeared satisfied with his wife, so he was not about to divorce her, and there was no divorce for an unhappy woman.

Over the years Abigail had learned to manage her unpleasant husband, but she wasn't the president of his fan club. She was well aware of his irascible disposition and his tendency to make rash decisions, for she had to live in constant readiness to counteract any foolish thing he might do.

If she wanted her household led in honoring and worshiping *Yahweh,* the God of Israel, she had learned a long time ago that she would have to be the one to do it.

THE LITTLE RED HEN

Ellen's and Abigail's conclusions are really parts of a lesson we all begin learning in childhood. For example, in the children's book, *The Little Red Hen*, the hen found some grains of wheat. Excitedly, she showed it to her friends—the pig, the goat, and the cat (or whatever animals were in your favorite version). She explained that they could plant these seeds, raise some wheat, have it ground into flour, and make bread for them to eat.

She asked who would help her plant the seeds.

"Not I," said the pig, goat, etc. You remember. They all made excuses why they could not help.

"Then I will plant the wheat myself," the little red hen declared. And she did.

The same scenario was repeated when the wheat was ready for harvesting, when it was ready to be taken to the mill, when it was time to bake the fresh-ground flour into bread. Each time the three friends had pressing engagements elsewhere.

Finally, the irresistible aroma of baking bread filled the air. The pig, the goat, and the cat drew near.

"Who will help me eat the bread?" the little red hen asked slyly, as she took the crusty loaves from the oven.

"I will," "I will," "I will," were the eager responses.

"Think again, you lazy good-for-nothings," said the little red hen. And she quoted Captain John Smith's edict to the colonists, "He who does not work, shall not eat." Or words to that effect. "My little chicks and I shall eat the bread." And they did.

Some versions say the little red hen was kind enough to share, but the moral of this story does not lie simply in the lesson the animals learned about working for rewards. It incorporates the commendable determination of the hen to get the job done, even if she had to do it all herself. And, with the good instincts God had given her, she did.

JAEL

Judges 4:17–22 tells us Jael was the wife of Heber, a Kenite, whose tribe enjoyed friendly relations with the king of Canaan, though Heber's ancestry could be traced from the line of Moses' brother-in-law, Hobab.

When the Israelite army pursued the Canaanite army through Kenite territory and destroyed them, the dreaded general, Sisera, escaped and headed straight for the Kenite's camp. Jael saw Sisera outside her tent and went out to meet him. "'Come, my lord, come right in,' she urged. 'Don't be afraid.' So he entered her tent, and she put a covering over him.'"

Sisera asked Jael to stand guard at the doorway of the tent. But Jael picked up a tent peg and a hammer and went quietly to him while he lay sleeping. She drove the peg through his temple, killing him.

The Bible doesn't tell us why Jael made the abrupt decision to kill Sisera, who had cruelly oppressed Israel for twenty years. It does not tell us why she took it upon herself to change the loyalties of the Kenite tribe from the Canaanite to the Hebrew cause. Surely it was her husband's place to make that far-reaching decision.

Heber wasn't there when the opportunity to eliminate Sisera arose, and Jael didn't wait for him to come home and tell her what to do. She made her decision and acted boldly upon it. Her fearless act led to Israel's freedom from Canaanite persecution for many years and earned her an honored place in the history of God's people.

A WOMAN'S STRENGTHS

Women today sometimes feel they must disguise their strengths to attract a man. "What man wants a woman who is smarter or stronger than he is?" we are warned. But David was not intimidated by the strengths he saw in Abigail. He realized her wisdom had prevented him from making a big political and spiritual mistake.

To kill a large portion of a tribe of Israel for personal revenge would have alienated that tribe later when he needed their support as leader of Israel. To seek vengeance by killing Nabal with his own hands would break God's commandment against murder and violate his own moral commitments. (He should have sought Abigail's counsel before he ordered Uriah's death in the sordid incident over Bathsheba.)

David saw Abigail's strengths as a balance to his own strengths and weaknesses. He could see that she exemplified all that was best in a woman, and that she brought out all that was best in him.

Ellen, too, had strengths her husband relied upon to keep their home and their social and spiritual obligations running smoothly with as little help from him as possible. Like Abigail, she spent a lot of time and effort covering up Ron's shortcomings before other people. She was ashamed to admit that her husband was not the spiritual head of their household, as she naively assumed was true of every other man in their church body.

What Ellen didn't realize was that she was not responsible for Ron's relationship with God, the church, or anybody else. Yes, it was her duty, whether or not he had been baptized, to try to be the example described in 1 Peter 3:1: "Wives ... be submissive to your husbands so that, if any of them do not believe the word, they may be won over without words by the behavior of their wives."

She will not be graded, however, on her success at nagging, cajoling, or shaming Ron into being the spiritual husband and father God meant him to be. Ron is the one who will have to stand before God and account for his failure to fulfill the role God has given him.

The children are a different matter. Both she and Ron will be accountable to God for bringing up their sons and daughters to have their own personal relationship with him. If Ron will not do his part, it is up to Ellen to fill that gap. She will have to do everything in her power to raise her children "in the fear and admonition of the Lord." I knew Ellen would give it all she had.

On a happier note she told me that at the meeting with Katie's teacher, she was frank about their beliefs and her distress at learning Katie was being taught something contrary to them. The teacher admitted she wasn't sure what she believed and was just quoting theories from the textbook and her college classes. Mrs. Jenkins promised to be more sensitive in the future but insisted that Katie learn not to argue publicly with her teacher. Ellen agreed to reinforce that.

The potential problem was solved for now, and Ron had not been required to step out of his comfort zone.

THE BITTER ROOT

Many people have stepped suddenly out of the ranks of the unconcerned and turned their lives over to God. Ron may yet seek a closer relationship with God and become exactly what

Ellen has always dreamed he would be, but she has no guarantee of that.

Ron may never try to know and love God the way she does, or share that part of her life completely. His excuse at the moment is that he is too busy earning a living for the family. However, when he retires, he may fill his time with hobbies, with the retired men's "breakfast club," with projects and puttering. In short he probably won't spend his new free time in Bible study or church activities. He may never make an all-out effort to become the man of God she has desired for so long.

GREAT EXPECTATIONS

I've heard it said that true love is an acceptance of all that is, has been, will be, and will not be. It's the "for better or for worse" no starry-eyed bride ever thinks will turn out to be the latter. I've also heard that just because someone doesn't love you the way you want them to, doesn't mean they don't love you with all they have.

Sometimes we expect too much of other people. When I was a young bride, I expected my husband to fulfill all my needs. I based my sense of worth on being number one in his life. But I expected more than any other human being ever was meant to provide.

Like Ellen, I had to learn it is not someone else's fault if he does not fit the idealistic image I have created for him. Each person is his or her own unique self, created by God that way, just as I was.

I cannot remold anyone into what I need or want him to be. Neither can you. If we could, then we would be God.

BACK TO ABIGAIL

David was so impressed by Abigail's wisdom and courage that he knew he wanted that woman to become his wife. And that, as Paul Harvey would say, is the rest of the story.

Abigail leaned back against the tree trunk behind the stone bench where she sat, watching the bees work among the flowering herbs. Across the way a bird poured out its heart to its maker. *It is pleasant here in the shade of the garden,* Abigail thought, *with no loud voice upbraiding me or one of the servants.*

When she had told Nabal of the incident with David, he had a seizure and dropped like a stone. Ten days later he suffered another spell and died. She saw to it that he had the funeral befitting his position and that the required days of mourning were observed. Yet she did not grieve for Nabal. Long ago he had killed any affection she might have had for him.

She did not know what she would do once Nabal's inheriting

kinsman came to claim his property. He wanted the house, of course, but he had invited her to stay there with him and his three wives. *And their ten rambunctious children.*

She had much jewelry that Nabal had given her over the years. Perhaps she would sell it and build a little cottage at the edge of the property, if the new owner agreed.

Her thoughts were interrupted by the appearance on the horizon of two men walking briskly toward her. She stood up and shaded her eyes with her hand. As they drew nearer, she could see that they were dressed like David's men.

Nabal cannot have offended him this time, she thought. What could be the purpose of this unexpected visit? Should she be alarmed?

The men bowed low before her. "Mistress," one of them said, "we bring you greetings from our master David. He has heard of your bereavement and wishes us to express his condolences."

Her eyebrows raised questioningly, and she bowed her head to hide the skeptical smile that touched her lips.

The other man laughed, his eyes sparkling with mischief. "Actually, mistress," he corrected, "David's words were: 'Praise be to the Lord who has upheld my cause against Nabal for treating me with contempt. He has kept his servant from doing wrong and has brought Nabal's wrongdoing down on his own head.'"

So he has, Abigail agreed silently. *But why, then, have you come?*

The other man gave his companion a warning look. "Mistress," he said seriously, "David also has sent us to you to take you to become his wife."

Abigail's heart stopped, then began to beat against her ribs like a dove trying to escape a trap. *This is no trap, though,* she told herself. *It's what I did not dare to dream while Nabal was alive.*

She knew David already had one wife, two if she counted Michal, Saul's daughter, whom the king had given to another man after he forced David to go into hiding. David would lead Israel someday, and he likely would have many wives. Still, that day when *Yahweh* had sent her to stop David from seeking vengeance with his own hands, had there not been an instant rapport between them? She had felt his admiration and respect, had read it in his beautiful dark eyes.

Abigail bowed to the men. "Here is your maidservant, ready to serve you and wash the feet of my master's servants," she answered humbly. First Samuel 25:42 says, "Abigail quickly got on a donkey and, attended by her five maids, went with David's messengers and became his wife."

Second Samuel 3:3 tells us Abigail bore David his second son, Kileab. We would hope she spent many happy years as one of David's most cherished, and certainly most respected, wives, whose wisdom helped guide him as he led, not only a large household, but a nation.

If you are in the situation of having to be the head of your household, let me share with you the verses that have guided me most of my life: "Trust in the Lord with all your heart and lean not on your own understanding; in all your ways acknowledge him, and he will make your paths straight" (Prov. 3:5–6).

In other words, don't make your own decisions without first seeking answers from his Word and through prayer. Wait for his confirmation. Acknowledge him, not only through the major expected ways like public confession of him as Savior and Lord and baptism, but in small things like the greeting cards you send, the business cards you carry, your interactions with friends and strangers as you go about your everyday life.

True to his word, he will direct your paths. He does mine, if I let him.

7

JOB'S WIFE

THEME: *Trust*

Scripture: Job 2:9; 42:12–17

She stood in the doorway of the house, looking out over the fields to where they rose into the hills. Where once thousands of sheep, oxen, camels, and donkeys had grazed, there now was nothing but emptiness.

She never would forget that terrible day when they had lost everything. First, a servant came to tell Job that the Sabeans had swooped down upon them, taken all 500 yoke of oxen and 500 donkeys and put the servants to the sword. He alone was left to bring Job the news.

While he was speaking, another servant ran in with the incredible news that fire had fallen from the sky and destroyed all 7,000 sheep and their shepherds. Only he was left to tell the story.

A third servant then arrived with the news that three bands of marauding Chaldeans had carried off all 3,000 camels and killed their herdsmen with the sword. Again, only the one servant had escaped to tell the tale.

Then the final devastating news: "Your sons and daughters were feasting and drinking wine at the home of the eldest when a mighty wind swept in from the desert and struck the four corners of the house. It collapsed on them, and they are dead," he said. "I am the only one escaped to tell you."

Her husband tore his robes, then shaved his head, and exclaimed, "Naked came I from my mother's womb, and naked I will depart. The Lord gave and the Lord has taken away; may the name of the Lord be praised."

May his name be cursed, she thought angrily. Only the Mighty God that Job worshipped so devoutly could have sent those winds from all four directions at once. He deliberately had crushed her children beneath the rubble of that house, and at the same time, he had crushed her heart beyond mending.

She knew the children liked holding feasts. Often she and Job were invited, but her husband would not take part in what he called debauchery. After each feasting had run its course, he would make offerings and have the children purified. Every morning, as surely as the sun arose, she would see Job out there at his altar offering burnt sacrifices for each son and daughter.

"Perhaps my children have sinned and cursed God in their hearts," he would say.

Job had been strong and robust, busy and content as he moved among his servants, the thousands of sheep and camels, the yokes of oxen, and the donkeys that had sent their commanding brays echoing through the hills.

She had known happiness then, when her children dwelt in fine houses close by and often came to visit. It had been easier to accept Job's God when her children flocked around her.

Now she looked out over the desolate land, bereft of the sounds of animals. There was only the mourning of a dove from the olive tree outside the kitchen garden and the soft bleating of one nanny goat that had been spared because she had been turned in to eat the tall grasses of the yard.

Only one of the four servants who had brought them the news of their devastation remained, along with one housemaid. Job had let the other servants go because there was nothing for them to do, and they could no longer afford to feed them.

From the chimney corner she heard Job moan. The sound grated down her spine. Not long after their world had fallen apart, her strong, healthy husband had broken out with sores all over his body, from the soles of his feet to the top of his head. His feet were so painful, he could barely walk on them. All he did was sit among the ashes and scrape his sores with a piece of broken pottery.

His skin hung from his bones like a hand-me-down from an older brother. She had fixed him nourishing foods and begged him to eat, but the best he could do was to painfully swallow some gruel made from wheat and goat's milk.

How fortunate that she had made a pet of this one nanny goat and she had not been with the sheep and their shepherds in the fields when the fire fell from heaven. Now her milk was the only nourishment that kept Job alive.

Maybe it wasn't so fortunate, she thought bitterly. *Would he not be better off resting peacefully among his ancestors in their burial cave?* Every moan of agony that escaped his lips pierced through her like a sword. She had loved this man with all her heart, long before he was the richest and most powerful man in the east. She still loved him, though he had lost everything.

Job moaned softly, calling on his God for mercy. *Mercy?* she thought bitterly. *It may have been common thieves who stole our oxen, donkeys, and camels. It may even have been some strange natural lightning or fiery hail that fell on our sheep and shepherds. But it was your God, Job, who killed our children and sent this curse on you.*

Suddenly, she could stand it no longer. She moved over to stand in front of him. "Are you still holding onto your integrity?" she cried. "Curse God and die."

Job reached out with one blistered finger to wipe away the tears that flooded down her cheeks, though the salty tears must have stung his sores. "Ah, beloved," he admonished her, "you are talking like a foolish woman. Shall we accept good from God, and not trouble?"

She shook her head, and walked away to stand in the doorway with her back to him, letting the tears fall. Then her tear-blurred vision focused on four men walking toward the house.

"Job, you have company," she warned, wondering what the men wanted. Since disaster had claimed them, not one friend, not one relative, not even one of his brothers had come to comfort Job. It was as though they feared that his misfortune might be contagious, that his curse might reach out for them.

She blinked away the tears and was able to recognize the three older men as Job hobbled painfully out to meet them. They had been her husband's friends for years—Eliphaz from the town of Teman, Bildad from over at Shuah, and Zophar who lived at Naamah. She didn't recognize the younger one.

"In the name of Almighty God, I would not have recognized you, Job!" she heard Eliphaz cry when the men had drawn near enough to speak.

"Nor I!" exclaimed Bildad.

Zophar stood staring at Job and shaking his head.

The young man she did not recognize said nothing, but he joined the three older men as they began to wail, tear their robes, and throw dust upon their heads in sympathy.

"This is Elihu," Eliphaz finally introduced the young man, "the son of Barachel, the Buzite."

Job bowed painfully in acknowledgement then sank weakly to his haunches. The four men squatted to the ground around him, apparently unable to think of anything more to say.

She went listlessly back to the stew she was preparing, though she didn't know why she bothered. It was unlikely that Job would eat it.

As time for the evening meal drew near, the men still were sitting there, none of them saying a word, including Job. She took them some of the stew and some fresh-baked bread. All but Job ate, silently. When she finally went to bed that night, they still were there, sitting on the ground, saying nothing.

She glanced out the door, knowing what she would see. For seven days and seven nights now Job's four visitors had sat with him, saying nothing. The tragedy they found here had rendered them speechless.

Suddenly, she heard Job cry out, "Why did I not perish at birth, and die as I came from the womb?"

Then Eliphaz responded. His voice was low, and she could not hear everything he said, but she caught the words, "Blessed is the man whom God corrects; so do not despise the discipline of the Almighty."

"If only my anguish could be weighed and all my misery be placed on the scales. It would surely outweigh the sands of the seas," Job sighed, when Eliphaz's long speech ended.

She tuned out the rest of Job's now familiar lament. Though she had great sympathy for the miserable condition of his body, she had no more words of comfort for her husband. Although her own body bore no visible sores or scars, her soul was pocked with wounds.

Having less butter for her bread, having no fine new wools to spin, having no soft leather to comfort her feet was nothing. *I spit upon such trivial things. But how can I bear never seeing my children again? I will never stop missing them. I will never stop seeing them everywhere I turn, hearing their voices, their laughter.*

They were such laughing children, she remembered, looking out over the garden and the fields where they once had played, *and they*

*enjoyed each other so much, my seven handsome sons and three beau-
tiful daughters.*

She wished they hadn't enjoyed each other's company so much.
Perhaps then one or two of them would not have been in that
house and would have been spared the destroying winds. *The winds
of* El Gibbor, *the mighty God, the one who has no mercy for a grieving mother's heart.*

Suddenly, she saw the bony hand of death beckoning. "Leave
this valley of tears," it seemed to say. "End this agony."

I could do that, she thought. There were poisons she had mixed
for the rats that raided the grain bins. It might bring a painful
death, but it would be quicker and less painful than living out her
days alone. Her children were gone, and surely Job would soon follow them.

*Even if there is nothing after death but the silence of the grave, at
least, there would be peace. What have I to keep me here?*

LAURA

I knew Laura and Nathan well, though those are not their real
names. They were a perfect match—she creative and ethereal, he
practical and down-to-earth. Throughout the fifteen years of their
marriage, he had always been there, supporting her as she finished
her degrees, encouraging her in her career, taking care of the mun-
dane things as she soared above them.

He was the wind beneath her wings, and his death when they were in their early thirties nearly destroyed her. *If God loved me, he would not have taken Nathan,* she thought bitterly.

She and Nathan had witnessed for the Lord in many places. "For God so loved the world …," they had sung, his perfect tenor or bass (he could sing them both) blending with her soft soprano.

What fools we made of ourselves. How stupid we were to believe there was a God who loved us. How naive to stand up and proclaim the love of a God who would not lift a finger to save Nathan, who loved him with all his heart.

"Whatever God does with me is all right," Nathan had insisted as he battled the cancer invading his body. "If he heals me, it's okay. If I die, it's okay. I am willing for him to do whatever he wants with me."

She had watched him waste away from the merciless disease and the debilitating treatments that had robbed him of any quality of life those last weeks.

He had maintained his faith, his trust in his God until the end, and what good had it done him? He lay buried in the cemetery among all those who had gone before—the trusting and the unaware, the faithful and the unbelievers.

"I don't believe in God," she said aloud. The rebellious words echoed through the empty house and trembled in her mind, but she reaffirmed them. *He either doesn't exist, or, worse, he doesn't care.* Suddenly, the temptation of escape spread through her mind. *I have no children to hold me here. Why should I go on suffering this grief, this despair when I can end it so easily?*

The doctors had prescribed chemical comforters to get her

through the grieving period. An overdose of one or all of them would suffice.

What will I do about my family? she wondered. *Call one of them and confess my plans? It would take any one of them at least an hour to get here. By then, it would all be over.* Still, one of them might manage to stop her some way. Once she made up her mind, she did not intend to be stopped.

A note, she decided. *That would be best.* They would find it with her body, after it was too late to change things. They would grieve, but they had their own lives to live. They would go on. And surely they would understand how desperate she was, how hopeless.

"You cannot take your own life and then ask forgiveness for it," she could imagine Mom saying. "You will spend eternity in hell."

There was a time when she had believed that. Now she wasn't so sure. If she no longer believed in God, then she no longer believed in hell. And even if she did still believe in a cruel Mark Twain kind of God who enjoyed watching his creatures suffer, she wasn't convinced that even he would punish her for ending such a painful existence.

"We will leave him in the hands of the God who made and loves him," she recalled a preacher saying once at the funeral of a suicide. *Well, that brings me right back to where I started,* she thought. *If there was a God who loved me, he would not have taken Nathan from me.*

The silence of the empty house rose up around her. Everywhere she looked, she saw the two of them. Over there, they had watched a movie, curled up on the couch together. There, they had sat in separate chairs, reading, the light glinting off

Nathan's blond head bowed over his book. Here, in the kitchen, they had cooked together, and eaten at this small table, looking out over the gardens, planning for the next season.

A scream built inside her. She jumped up and threw her half-empty teacup into the sink, hearing it shatter, but not caring. *I've got to do something soon. I cannot bear to spend another empty day or lonely night in this house.*

Nathan's insurance was generous. She could pay all her bills and have a great deal left. Perhaps she would flee from her agony, go to Europe or England or even Australia. *Anywhere away from here. I simply cannot stand it any longer.*

Yet, deep down, she knew that running from her grief would not assuage it. What was the old saying? "Everywhere I go, there I am." There would be no escaping her memories, her bitter thoughts.

Laura went down the hall to the bathroom. Her hand shook as she opened the medicine cabinet ...

UNDERSTANDING JOB'S WIFE

The book of Job may have been written by Job himself at some time during the 140 years he lived after the events recorded there, or it may have been passed down as a folk tale with poetic additions by some later writer. Don't we wish, though, that whoever wrote it had added more about Mrs. Job in those later years?

Job's family probably lived 300 to 500 years before the time of

Abraham. There was no king in the land in these early days of the patriarchs, and Job was the richest, most powerful man in the east.

Moses had not yet been born, and there were no Ten Commandments. There was no Law, no tabernacle (much less a temple), and there was no Aaronic priesthood to teach God's laws. Yet Job had the laws of God written clearly on his heart. No one knows how he got them, but he surely shared them with his wife and children. The children apparently had paid them little heed, or Job would not have felt compelled to continually make sacrifices for them.

Perhaps Mrs. Job, however, had been persuaded to believe in her husband's God. If so, the tragedies they faced must have seemed like betrayal by a God they had served devotedly. Like Laura, she may have felt that if God loved them, he would not have allowed them to suffer so. Consequently, she became bitter, as evidenced by her desperate cry to Job, "Curse God and die."

Job's wife has been used for centuries as an example of a hardhearted shrew who turned against her husband when he was down. She had enjoyed the good times, but when he was no longer any use to her, when he had become a burden, she wanted him out of the way.

In fact, the truth may have been the opposite. She may have grieved as she watched him diminish from the man she had known to a gaunt caricature of himself. Her desperate words could have come, not from an uncaring heart, but from one that cared so deeply she could no longer bear to see him suffer.

On the other hand, she may have blamed her husband for the things his God had brought upon them. She may have lashed out to inflict pain because her own pain was so great. It must have been difficult to be demoted from the equivalent of the queen or first lady to the wife of a pauper who sat in the ashes scraping his sores with broken pottery.

Wrapped in her own grief at the loss of her children, she may simply have grown weary of hearing Job's endless moaning, accompanied by what she considered senseless praise of the one who had caused his sorrows.

Job, though, never turned away from God. He felt that God, for some unknown reason, had turned against him. He asked why. He begged to see God face to face to plead his case. But his bottom line remained, "Though he slay me, yet will I trust him."

Most of us react more like Mrs. Job or Laura. If life doesn't turn out the way we expect or think it should and we find ourselves in a desperate situation, we feel that God has abandoned us, that he either doesn't exist or doesn't love us. Been there? Me, too.

THE PRECIOUS PRESENT

Laura didn't follow through with her thoughts of suicide that day, but she shared them with me. "I haven't decided when or how," she said, "but I'm pretty sure that's what I'm going to do." Unwilling to leave her alone in that state of mind, but obligated to implement a conference for my employer, I insisted Laura accompany me.

God truly works in mysterious ways. The keynote speaker at

the conference based his talk on the little book, *The Precious Present*, by *New York Times* best-selling author Spencer Johnson. Laura half listened as he told the story of an old man who shares with a little boy the secret to true happiness, which it takes the boy a lifetime to understand.

In summary the secret is that it is all right to reminisce, to visit the past in memory, even to treasure it, but we must realize the past is over and we can no longer live in it. On the other hand, it is all right to look toward the future and prepare for it, but we must borrow neither trouble nor pleasure from it. It is not here yet. It may never come. We must learn to live in the present—*The Precious Present*—to savor each moment of life as it comes.

The words of that little story penetrated Laura's fog of misery. She began to see that her time with Nathan was a closed chapter in the book of her life, and now she must move on to the next chapter.

Today, Laura enjoys a busy career that has brought her many honors and rewards. Nathan is a beautiful part of her past that she sometimes visits wistfully, even tearfully, but she no longer lives there.

DARRELL

A similar pain to Laura's touched my brother Darrell and his lovely wife, Susan. They were charter members of their church, where he

was an active deacon, teacher, and counselor. A successful businessman, he gave sacrificial amounts of money to the Lord's work. He
and Susan witnessed to the lost, fed the hungry, visited the prison-
ers, ministered to the sick, comforted the mourners.

Without warning Darrell was diagnosed with a virulent form
of cancer. Trusting God for a favorable outcome, he submitted to
the drastic surgery that removed his esophagus and part of his
stomach. He endured the intensive radiation and chemo treatments the doctors recommended.

As Darrell endured excruciating pain and nausea for months,
with a daunting prognosis, he and Susan spent hours on their
knees. Nevertheless, things just seemed to go from bad to worse.
New medical problems paraded through their lives. The business
he had thought to resume in a couple of months, languished.

"Somebody else will have to pray for us," Darrell and Susan
admitted in exhaustion. "Our prayers are bouncing off the ceiling."

Like Job, Darrell, suffering and depressed, felt that God had
turned against him, and he could not understand why.

WHY?

We are told in the beginning of the book of Job that Job's suffering
was a result of Satan's challenge to God. It has been said that Job
was the innocent victim of God's confidence in him. Job had no
way of understanding that, and we have no evidence that God ever

explained to him why he had gone through such agony, though Job asked him many times.

Likewise, Darrell never knew in this life why he endured such suffering. Was there something God wanted to teach him? Was he testing him? Had Satan asked to "sift him like wheat" as he had with Peter? Had Satan sought permission from God to take everything Darrell had to see if he would "curse you to your face" as he had with Job? Was the enemy trying to rob Darrell of his salvation by pushing him to the point where he gave up on God?

First Peter 5:8 says, "Your enemy the devil prowls around like a roaring lion looking for someone to devour." His favorite target seems to be the faithful Christian. Just when he or she seems to be achieving that longed-for relationship with the Lord, just when he or she is most effective in the Lord's work, Satan pounces. Without warning. Without mercy.

For reasons we don't understand, God allows Satan to afflict us. Sometimes he takes the most important thing in a believer's life, like taking Nathan from Laura. Sometimes he takes everything, like he did with Job, or inflicts terrible pain and suffering, like Darrell endured. Sometimes he subtly engineers great disappointments that turn to hopelessness, as with Ellen in our chapter on Abigail.

Slyly, he leads his prey to that place where she believes God has abandoned her. "He doesn't care about you or your brother," he whispered to me when my prayers for Darrell seemed to rebound from a brass heaven and the Scriptures I tried to read didn't even register.

We all are made of the same vulnerable clay. Some can endure more heat than others. All, though, are susceptible to the cunning lies of Satan when the suffering has exhausted our mental, physical, and spiritual resources. Even Jesus cried from the cross, "My God! My God! Why have you forsaken me?"

Thank God, Darrell and Susan clung to their faith until the end, nine months later, when Darrell went home to be with the Lord.

Whatever our strengths or weaknesses, whatever our circumstances, we all must come to that quiet place of resignation where we let go of the struggle and say with Job and Nathan and Darrell, "Though he slay me, yet will I trust him."

AND WE MUST PRAISE HIM

What? When the circumstances are bleak and the pain is unbearable, when the loss is more than we can face and the future is terrifying, we must praise him? When he hasn't protected us from calamities or brought us out of them? When our prayers hit the ceiling and bounce back? Praise him? How? Why? Hebrews 13:15 says, "Through Jesus, therefore, let us continually offer to God a sacrifice of praise—the fruit of lips that confess his name."

To praise God after he has answered our prayers is gratitude. To praise him before he answers them is faith. When we don't feel like praising, that's when we must offer up a "sacrifice of praise." It isn't easy. That's what makes it a sacrifice. Likewise,

Isaiah 61:3 encourages us to put on "a garment of praise instead of a spirit of despair."

WE ARE NOT IN CHARGE

I love living in a democracy. I love being able to elect the leaders of my country, my state, my community. I love having some power over the way they run things. But the kingdom of God is not a democracy. We don't have a vote, and we have only those rights guaranteed by his Word, those promises that begin, "If you will ..." and end, "Then I will ..." We have no other guarantees, no other Bill of Rights.

When God took Nathan, Laura had no say in the matter. God was not snatching something away from her to which she had exclusive rights forever. God had loaned him to her for a little while. He did not have to ask her permission to take him back. And it wasn't because he didn't love her that he did so. The plans he had for Nathan included taking him home at a young age. Why? Only God knows. The plans he had for Laura included these latter years without Nathan. Why? Again, only God knows.

When the doctors told Darrell he would die of the cancer ravaging his body, he said simply, "Well, everybody has to die of something." He knew he was not guaranteed a pain-free existence or a life without troubles just because he was trying to serve the Lord.

The fact that we want to serve the Lord seems to incite Satan to attack us, but it also gives God the opportunity to use whatever he knows it will take to mold us into the kind of servant he wants. It is the irritating, distressful sand in the oyster that makes a pearl. It is the fire that removes the dross from the silver.

BACK TO JOB'S WIFE

At the end of the story we find Job receiving double the material blessings he had before calamity hit, and the same number of children he had lost—seven sons and three strikingly beautiful daughters. We are told that Job enjoyed his children and grandchildren to the fourth generation.

What if Job had given in to his wife's urging that he "curse God and die"? What if he had let her help him with an assisted suicide? What if he had gambled on God forgiving him because he was in such pain, and then discovered, once it was too late, that he had forfeited his place in heaven? At least, as it turned out, he would have missed the greatest blessings of his life on earth, and so would she.

Since the Bible does not mention that Job had a different wife to share all these renewed blessings, it must have been the same old Mrs. Job who enjoyed this second wave of prosperity and bore him these ten new children.

If she had remained bitter and prone to curse God, surely he would have replaced her. It is likely, though, that she began her journey back to faith as she listened in on Job's longed-for face-to-face encounter with Almighty God.

꒦꒷

Job's wife had listened to Eliphaz preach for days on his belief that God only punishes bad men, not good ones.

Bildad had insisted that "even the moon and the stars are not clean in God's sight, so how can he who is born of woman be clean?"

Zophar had urged Job to admit his faults so that God could forgive him. "God exacts of you less than your guilt deserves," he exclaimed indignantly.

Job is a good man, she thought. *He has committed none of the sins of which these so-called friends accuse him. Never has he abused a servant or turned away a weary traveler. He has provided for the widows and orphans. He has championed the cause of the oppressed.*

"Doubtless you are the people, and wisdom will die with you," Job shouted suddenly. "I have a mind as well as you; I am not inferior to you. Who does not know all these things?"

His sarcasm reminded her of the old Job and the days when he and his three friends often had enjoyed a heated debate—over anything from the value of a camel or a sheep to the ways of the

Almighty. Sometimes she had feared they would come to blows, but they always parted friends.

"To your sin, you add rebellion," the young man, Elihu, now accused, pointing out that God chastises in order to enlighten the soul and bring about a more intimate relationship with himself.

As she waited to hear what Job would answer, suddenly the wind rose, thunder rolled, and lightning flashed. Then a voice spoke out of the storm, turning her legs to jelly and causing her to sink to her knees. She saw that Job and the four men had prostrated themselves.

"Who is this that questions my wisdom with such ignorant words?" the voice roared. "Brace yourself like a man, because I have some questions for you, and you must answer them. Where were you when I laid the foundations of the earth? Tell me, if you know so much." And he spoke of the mighty works of creation—of the earth and the sea, of day and night, of the creatures with which he had filled them all.

Then the voice demanded, "Do you still want to argue with the Almighty? You are God's critic, but do you have the answers?"

She saw Job raise his head and heard him answer shakily, "I am nothing—how could I ever find the answers? I will cover my mouth with my hand. I have said too much already. I have nothing more to say."

Again the voice spoke to Job out of the storm. "Brace yourself like a man, because I have some questions for you, and you must answer them. Will you discredit my justice and condemn me just to prove you are right?" And he spoke of the mighty things he had made—of behemoth and leviathan, of snow and hail and lightning bolts—and the way they all obeyed him.

"You asked, 'Who is this that questions my wisdom with such ignorance?'" Job confessed then. "It is I—and I was talking about things I knew nothing about, things far too wonderful for me.... I had only heard about you before, but now I have seen you with my own eyes. I take back everything I said, and I sit in dust and ashes to show my repentance" (Job 38–42 NLT).

Perhaps Mrs. Job understood with Job that faith in God has little to do with circumstances, blessings, or answers to intellectual questions. It comes from a revelation of God himself, which demands nothing less in return than the humble confession Job made.

Whether our initial encounter with God occurs in a crash of thunder as it did with Job, in a flash of light as it did to Paul, or as a "still, small voice" in the inner recesses of our own minds, the only possible response is an acknowledgment like Job's of who he is (the Creator) in comparison to who we are (the created).

No more questions. No more debate. No more justifying. No more agonizing over fairness. No more struggle to understand why. Just a humble surrender to the superiority of the Creator over his creation.

THE THINGS GOD HAS CREATED ARE WONDERFUL, BUT …

When he was about eight years old, my son attended a summer day camp that had a wonderful program involving the children with animals and nature. What I did not know was that the camp's director each year allotted one week to teaching the beliefs of her religion.

One day, when I asked my son if he still was enjoying the camp, he said, "I love it when we feed and play with the animals, but I don't much like it this week. I don't say those chants 'cause I don't know what they mean. I just mumble something and pretend."

Upon further questioning I learned that the director had been teaching the children to chant, "The Earth is our Mother. The Sky is our Father. The Trees are our Brothers. The Animals are our Friends …," and leading them in worship of these created things. Thank God, my son, even at this early age, knew that only the Creator is worthy of worship.

OUR RESPONSE

James 4:10 says, "Humble yourselves before the Lord, and he will lift you up."

Psalm 50:15 (TLB) says, "I want you to trust me in your times of trouble, so I can rescue you, and you can give me glory."

Isaiah 49:23 (NCV) says, "Anyone who trusts in me will not be disappointed."

He may restore health and prosperity, as he did for Job. He may return emotional balance and lead into new and exciting adventures, as he did for Laura. He may, as he did with Darrell and Nathan, simply take us home.

No matter what his plans are for me, no matter what desperate circumstances may come my way, I hope I will be strong enough to declare with Job, "Though he slay me, yet will I trust him."

8

THE INNKEEPER'S WIFE

THEME: *Self-Esteem*

Scripture: Luke 2

*C*lutching her shawl around her with her right hand and carrying the jar of oil in her left, she eased her way through the haggling shoppers, the smelly shepherds, the burly Roman centurions. Daylight was fading, and she did not want to be caught in the street when night fell, not with all these strangers in town.

Her husband loved the mob the Roman emperor's census had brought to town, all these descendants of David who had come to register. The inn was overflowing. There wasn't a single room—or even part of a room—left to rent. He even had given their own bedchamber to a wealthy couple, and they were sleeping on a mat in the storage room.

She hated the crowds. She longed for the days when the town would return to the sleepy little village it had been, when the residents of Bethlehem would once again go about their business, free of the busy Roman world.

She was used to the shepherds. They came every year when the winds grew cold to pasture their flocks in the fields nearest Bethlehem, shopping for food among the market stalls and drinking wine at the cafés. They were unwashed and unkempt, and some of the merchants complained that they stole from them. They were of little concern to her, though, for shepherds neither slept at the inn nor stole from it.

It was rumored that among the strangers in town were those who stole from the shepherds—fat lambs to roast over their camp fires. She was sure it was true. Many of those who must register for the census were very poor, traveling miles on foot, eating what they could find, camping in every open spot to obey this latest of Caesar's whims.

Rich or poor, all of them are a nuisance, she thought, *pushing and shoving their way through the marketplace, filling the air with their raucous voices, their curses.*

Worse, Roman centurions paraded in front of every shop, even the synagogue, watching the Jews with their cynical eyes and mocking smiles, treating village women like women of the street. Once, she had grieved over the fact that no one noticed her, but in the present circumstances, this was a blessing.

Lost somewhere in the middle of a large family, buried under menial tasks and hand-me-down clothing, she had often felt invisible. The eldest got attention. The youngest got attention. The prettiest got attention. The loudest got attention. She was none of those.

Convinced that she would never have an offer of marriage, she had been relieved when the middle-aged innkeeper had approached her father a few months after the death of his wife. She had known the man was motivated by his need of a mother for his three little boys, but she wanted a husband and a home of her own like her sisters and the other girls of the village.

As she hurried through the outer gate and into the inn, shutting the door firmly behind her, she could hear her husband calling, "Deborah!" His voice sounded exasperated, as though he might have called her several times. When he saw her, he said impatiently, "Deborah, we need more wine and cheese for our guests. Quickly!"

She hurried to the kitchen, sliced cheese and bread and arranged it on a tray, thinking how ironic it was that she had been named for Deborah, the famous judge of Israel who had led their army to victory in the old days. Obviously, none of the well-known bravery and boldness of Deborah had come with the name.

"Deborah!" The voice was growing angry.

She grabbed a skin of wine and the tray and fairly ran to the front room of the inn. "I'm sorry," she murmured, as she set the tray on the table and began pouring wine into the empty *ewers*. "I had to go to the market for more oil for the lamps," she explained, not daring to look into his eyes.

She felt she should curtsy and call him "Master." It was the way she always had felt toward her husband. She had washed and mended, cooked and cleaned, raised his children, met all the expectations of a man who knew what he wanted and expected to get it instantly. He wasn't a cruel man, but he was her master, as surely as if he had bought her on the auction block.

It had been nearly the same with the children. The scarcity of their visits now that they were grown and on their own only confirmed what she always had suspected—she was little more to them than a source of meals, clothing, and a clean place to sleep. Even the extra maids and cooks her husband had hired for this expected influx of travelers had little respect for their mistress. If they hadn't known they would have to answer to her husband, she doubted that one of them would have obeyed a thing she said.

If I were gone from the world, it would make no difference at all, she thought. *Others could be hired to do my duties. The small space I occupy would be closed over as quickly and as surely as the hole left in the wash basin when I remove my hands from the water.*

I am as empty as this wineskin, she thought, as she returned to the storage room for more. *No one even sees me. I might as well be invisible. If I did not hurt when I am pinched, I would not believe I exist.*

Suddenly, a man appeared in the doorway. "Sir, I must have a room," he said to her husband. "My wife is expecting a child at any moment. I must have a bed for her."

Her husband gave a wry laugh and shook his head. "The inn is filled to capacity," he said. "I couldn't give you a room if I wanted to." *Which I don't,* his face said plainly. The man's clothing marked him as a poor man, and Deborah knew her husband was thinking: *Peasant. No money.*

"But, sir, I will pay your price," the man begged, his dark eyes filled with desperation. "I must have a room."

"Then you must have it somewhere else," the Innkeeper answered. "The inn is full, I tell you. Now be off. Can't you see I am busy?"

Deborah eased to the doorway and looked out. A woman sat on a donkey outside. As Deborah watched, she bent double, clutching her body with both hands.

She is in labor, Deborah thought. *Surely there is somewhere we can put her, at least until her child is born.* She knew, though, that it wasn't possible. Even the stables under the inn were filled with people.

She will have to deliver her baby in the streets or in the fields, she thought. *How awful.*

She never had experienced the birth of a child, though she had raised her husband's three until they were grown and gone. She had assisted the midwife at births. She knew this woman would need boiling water and a sharp knife. She would need salt, then oil to rub down the newborn. She would need swaddling cloths and a clean place to lay the child.

All at once she remembered the small cave behind the inn that they used as a stable when the inn was full. It held only their own donkey and two milk goats now. It was a poor place, but it was shelter from the wind and it would only take a small fire to warm the snug space within the rock walls. There was a manger, too, which could be used as a cradle.

She hurried to her husband and whispered the idea in his ear, telling him of the woman's pitiful condition. He stared at her a moment, and she could see a flickering of compassion struggling against his irritation.

"Stranger," he called then, "come back." Deborah could not hear what her husband said when the man approached, but she saw despair migrate across the man's face and settle in his dark eyes. How he must hate having to tell his wife she would be bearing her child in a stable, but surely it would be better than the street or the field.

Straightening his shoulders, the man nodded. "I am grateful for your kindness, sir," he said. "Where do I find this stable?"

"I will show you," Deborah offered quickly, then felt her face flush at her boldness. "I will only be a moment," she promised her husband, but he already had turned toward a new arrival.

She grabbed her shawl from the hook by the door and went out ahead of the man. She heard the woman moan softly as they drew near the donkey.

"Mary, *yekarah*, I am sorry, but there is no room in the inn. The crowds …"

"Oh, Joseph, what shall we do? The child is coming."

"The innkeeper has kindly offered us his stable, *yekarah*. It is the best we can do at the moment. This good woman will take us there."

Deborah envied the easy way he called his wife "dear." She could not remember anyone ever calling her such an endearment, even as a child.

"Hurry, then," Mary urged, her eyes wide and dark with pain. A little moan escaped her. "Oh, please hurry."

Inside the cave Deborah helped Joseph settle Mary on a bed of clean straw, which he covered with his own cloak.

How gentle he is with her. How concerned for her suffering. I would gladly endure the pain of childbirth for a man who would look at me with that adoration in his eyes.

Then there would be the precious little one, the baby who would surely love his mother above all others, at least until he found a wife of his own. Or it might be a little girl who would love her mother as she had loved hers. This sweet Mary, though, she was sure would not shrug off her little girl's embrace or respond with a reminder of some chore waiting to be done.

She could hear her husband shouting her name from inside the inn. As she ran to obey, she cried. *Oh,* Yahweh, *I am so lonely. So empty. Will there never be someone who loves me, not for what I can provide, but for who I am?*

ALICE

Our informal counseling session wasn't going well. The young lady I'll call Alice knew she was intelligent and had been blessed with talents. She just didn't believe hers measured up to those of her older sister, Karen. In her mind nothing she did was good enough.

I tried to tell her she didn't need to compete with Karen. She was attractive. She had her own special abilities. She had a sweet personality that drew children and older people to her like hummingbirds to nectar. But she couldn't see it.

"It's not Karen's fault," she said. "She's a good sister, and I want her to be happy," she insisted. "It's just that, all my life, I've been compared to my older sister and found wanting.

"'Are you as smart as your sister?' the teachers asked me when

I entered their classes two years after Karen," she recalled. "Boys always begged, 'Introduce me to your sister.'"

She sighed. "Even my parents groan, 'Why can't you be like your sister?' when I do something stupid—which is often—or when my grades fall below Karen's high benchmark."

She wasn't like Karen, though. That much was obvious. Her thick, dark hair was not fair and curly. Her cat-green eyes were not wide and blue. They looked almost nothing alike. People meeting them for the first time always seemed amazed to learn that they were sisters.

"Karen's hand-me-downs never look as good on me as they did on her. And the dates Karen gets me always turn into disasters."

Still, I knew she'd rather have a hand-me-down outfit of Karen's than a brand new one. She would even rather have a hand-me-down boyfriend than choose one for herself. To Alice everything seemed especially blessed if it had belonged to Karen first.

It wasn't as though Karen lorded it over her. She was always the first to point out Alice's talents and try to encourage her to use them. I had heard her raving over Alice's drawings, telling her she would be the next Norman Rockwell. I had heard her applaud Alice's efforts to accompany the songs she wrote on their dad's old guitar, begging her to join the church praise team.

"Yeah, right," Alice laughed ruefully. "Like I'm going to get up there in front of all those people and hear my voice turn into a terrified squeak. Anyway, after a standing-ovation solo by Karen, who would want to hear her little sister's mediocre offerings?"

"Mediocre," she said now. "That's the word for me. Being a part of this talented family, I can do a number of things fairly well, but I shine at nothing. If I suddenly dropped off the face of the earth, it would be a while before anybody noticed I was gone."

When I tried to deny that, she shrugged. "That's just the way things are," she said. "The way they will always be."

THE VELVETEEN RABBIT

Like the title character in Marjorie Williams' little story, *The Velveteen Rabbit*, we all want to be *Real*.

"It doesn't happen all at once," the Skin Horse told the Velveteen Rabbit as they spoke of that strange and wonderful nursery magic that transforms special toys into *Real*. The Horse explained the pains of becoming real, that include having the child rub off most of your hair, lose your eyes, and pull on your joints until they are droopy. But, despite the pain, "When a child loves you for a long, long time, not just to play with, but *really* loves you," the Skin Horse concluded with awe, "then you become *Real*."

For some unfathomable reason, the Creator of the universe loved me, really loved me, even though down through the years, I had allowed my relationship with him to become shabby and had relegated him to a back shelf of outgrown abstractions.

Then I became aware that on a starlit night some 2,000 years ago, in the reality of a musty cow stall, he became *Emmanuel*—God with us. And according to John 1:12, "To all who received him, to those who believed in his name, he gave the right to become children of God."

In other words, through the strange and wonderful "magic" of his love, as you and I become more and more aware of the One "in whom we live and move and have our being," we become *Real*. We develop that relationship with God through Jesus Christ that makes us really alive, not just going through the motions. Jesus said in John 10:10, "I am come that they may have life, and that they might have it more abundantly" (KJV), or as the NIV puts it "to the full."

UNDERSTANDING THE INNKEEPER'S WIFE

Remember all those Christmas pageants with the burly innkeeper who gruffly turns away Mary and Joseph, then grudgingly offers them the use of his stable? Remember the innkeeper's wife? Of course not. She isn't there. Neither is the innkeeper. In the second chapter of Luke, the only gospel that relates the story of the stable and the shepherds, it simply says: "She wrapped him in cloths and placed him in a manger, because there was no room for them in the inn" (Luke 2:7).

There was an inn, so there must have been an innkeeper, right? And what innkeeper in his right mind would want to take on the task of running an inn the size of the one believed to have been in

Bethlehem at that time without a wife to handle the cooking and cleaning, the serving of food and drink, or at least the managing of the servants who did these tasks?

A successful innkeeper in those days would have had little trouble persuading some woman to marry him, or persuading her father to agree to the marriage, whether the girl was willing or not. Accustomed to being in control and having his every need met on demand, such a man might choose a wife who was docile and obedient, someone he could order around and expect to do his bidding without question.

Since the Bible is silent on the topic of a wife for our innkeeper at Bethlehem, like the mother of the Prodigal, our innkeeper's wife is a fictional character. Her hurts and needs are simply those common to many women in those long-ago days, as well as our own time.

Most of us, like the innkeeper's wife, aren't seeking greatness. We simply want to be recognized as a person, to be appreciated for who we are and what we do, to matter to somebody.

ZACCHAEUS

Zacchaeus, on the other hand, was an arrogant little chief tax collector in Jericho who had become wealthy by overcharging the taxpayers. When he heard Jesus was passing through, he wanted to see him. No doubt, he had heard stories about the miraculous things Jesus had done in other places.

"He wanted to see who Jesus was, but being a short man he could not, because of the crowd. So he ran ahead and climbed a sycamore-fig tree to see him, since Jesus was coming that way. When Jesus reached the spot, he looked up and said to him, 'Zacchaeus, come down immediately. I must stay at your house today'" (Luke 19:3–5).

Zacchaeus not only saw Jesus, but more importantly, Jesus saw him, and it changed Zacchaeus' life. When Zacchaeus saw himself reflected in Jesus' eyes, he *became* what Jesus saw and knew he could be.

UNIQUE AND SPECIAL

God could have made all flowers red, all autumn leaves yellow, all vegetables cabbage, all snowflakes round. Instead he created infinite variety, and—like snowflakes—he created each of us uniquely individual and special to him.

He doesn't expect me to be just like you. He doesn't want you to be just like someone else. He doesn't want us to wear someone else's armor that doesn't fit, like young David in 1 Samuel 17.

It doesn't matter to him if you are beautiful enough to be Miss America, or if you inherited your grandpa's big nose and your Aunt Thelma's crooked teeth. He doesn't care if your life is filled with exciting adventures or is spent scrubbing floors and cleaning toilets. He wants to be part of whoever and whatever you are.

Remember those T-shirts that pictured a little boy saying, "I'm somebody, 'cause God don't make no junk"? That statement may not be grammatically correct, but scripturally it is on target. Not one of us is a mistake.

> For we are God's masterpiece. He has created us anew in Christ Jesus, so that we can do the good things which he planned for us long ago. (Eph. 2:10 NLT)

> Are not five sparrows sold for two pennies? Yet not one of them is forgotten by God. Indeed, the very hairs of your head are all numbered. Don't be afraid; you are worth more than many sparrows. (Luke 12:6–7)

> For you created my inmost being; you knit me together in my mother's womb. I praise you because I am fearfully and wonderfully made.... My frame was not hidden from you when I was made in the secret place. When I was woven together in the depths of the earth, your eyes saw my unformed body. All the days ordained for me were written in your book before one of them came to be. (Ps. 139:13–16)

God knew you before you were a gleam in your father's eye. He isn't waiting for you to have your teeth straightened and plastic surgery on your nose so he can love you. He isn't waiting for you to change your personality. He sees and loves you just the way you are.

UNDER THE CURSE

But women are under the curse, right? You know, the one we inherited from Eve's little escapade in the garden. If you don't understand this, plenty of men out there will explain it to you. Even some women will agree that ever since the snake conned Eve, our punishment is to be second rate, subservient, and submissive.

For centuries women have been brainwashed into believing that they are supposed to sit down, shut up, mind the children, clean the building, and bring the pies. But if this is true, how do we explain Galatians 3:28: "There is neither Jew nor Greek, slave nor free, *male nor female*, for you are all one in Christ Jesus"?

Jesus made that clear when he sanctioned Mary's right to forego the housework Martha wanted her to do and, instead, encouraged her to sit at his feet and learn—right in there with the men. The significance of this quiet little episode related in Luke 10:38–43 often is overlooked. To think that women not only could, but should, learn was a groundbreaking concept in that patriarchal world.

Paul's admonitions that women not speak—much less teach or preach—in the church, are thought by many (men as well as women) to have been misinterpreted. It is likely that he was speaking of a specific circumstance in that specific church where specific women were causing trouble.

While Paul is often accused of being a chauvinist, his *high* regard for women in general is clearly seen as he speaks and writes well about the many women who shared his ministry: Priscilla (a coworker with Paul and her husband Aquila—Acts 18:1–26), Lydia (a leader in the church at Philippi—Acts 16:13–15; 40), Phoebe (a deaconess—Rom. 16:1), Euodia and Syntyche (laborers with Paul in the gospel—Phil. 4:2–3), Junias (a "notable apostle"—Rom. 16:7), and others.

Luke, also, writes in the book of Acts of the high esteem for women in the early church. The aim of both Paul and Luke was not to devalue the role of men, but to elevate the role of women to what God intended it to be.

For more than 2,000 years longer than necessary, women have been subjected to Eve's punishment. When Jesus died on that cross, he cancelled that ancient curse. He stomped on that old serpent's head and restored woman to the position she held before Eve met that wily snake. Helpmate, not servant. Equal, not inferior. Side-by-side, not three-steps-behind. In Christ it is men and women working together to promote the kingdom.

WASTING TIME

Likewise, Alice spent two decades too long in the shadow of her sister, unquestioningly accepting the role of second-best, voluntarily wearing the label of mediocrity. I grieved for her as I saw her miss opportunities, job promotions, relationships.

Then one day as Alice sat watching the Passion Play at her church on Easter, the narrator said, "If you had been the only person alive on the earth at that time, Jesus still would have died for you." Alice gasped and began to sob as she suddenly realized that Jesus had not extended a second-hand salvation to her. He had died for her! As she thought about how much Jesus truly loved her, how valuable she was to him as an individual, she finally understood that God never intended for her to be a carbon copy of her sister. Her relationship with him was one-on-one. She was exactly the person he wanted her to be.

You wouldn't recognize her now. She secured a top position with an out-of-state company in her chosen field, where she enjoys great respect among her peers. She has a husband who adores her. And, oh, yes, she sings alto on the praise team in her new church.

Some people spend years wallowing in regret and self-pity, reciting the wrongs done them in the past—the shameful circumstances of their births, the terrible childhoods they endured, the horror of the rejection of their peers, the misery their spouses inflicted upon them. Yada, yada, yada.

Of course, our background, our childhood experiences, and our life circumstances influence who we are. At some point, however, we cross the line to where we alone are responsible for what we become. Then, if we seek an encounter with God, he will love us, really love us, until we become, not what our circumstances have made us, but like Alice and Zacchaeus, all he intended us to be.

BACK TO DEBORAH

Our encounter is with the Lord who was born in a stable in Bethlehem, lived a sinless life, died for our sins, and conquered death for all of us. Deborah's might have been somewhat different—and yet remarkably similar.

Deborah meant to go straight back to the stable with supplies for the birth, but the demands of her husband and the press of duties kept her far into the night. Now the inn was still, except for the snoring of sleeping travelers, joined by her husband's snores from the storage room.

She knew it was too late now for boiling water and salt to rub the newborn, too late for swaddling cloths or a sharp knife to cut the cord. She hoped Mary had come prepared for all those needs.

Instead she packed a basket with cheese and bread, filled a small *ewer* with goat's milk, and took the last two covers from the cupboard. Wrapping her shawl around her, she slipped out the back door into the night.

The air was cold, stirred by a small wind, but the yard was nearly as light as day. She looked up and saw one uncommonly bright star hung low over the hill that held the stable. *I've never seen such a star,* she marveled as she drew near the entrance to the cave.

Inside, she could see the flicker of a fire and hear the murmur of voices. Then she realized the earthen room was filled with people, some spilling over outside.

"There were angels," she heard a man say.

"Many angels," another said.

"And they were all singing and praising God," the first voice added.

What on earth? Who are these men crowded into our stable? The place was hardly big enough to hold the poor couple she had led there earlier. She even had tied their own donkey and two goats outside to give them room.

She heard a woman's soft laughter. "Come and see him," she invited.

Deborah watched as the men pushed inside the cave, praising God in hushed voices. She knew now they were shepherds, from their clothing and from the unwashed, sheepfold smell of them. *They usually are a rough lot, those shepherds. I don't think I've ever heard one speak of angels or of praising God.*

"It is true, then," one of them exclaimed. "The angel said, 'You will find the babe wrapped in swaddling cloths, lying in a manger.' And here he is."

"My grandfather says the prophets have foretold that the Messiah will be born in Bethlehem," another declared.

"My father says he will come from the line of King David," a new voice said. "Surely you, sir, as well as every other visitor in Bethlehem, have come here to register because you are of that line."

"Praise be to *Yahweh*, God of Israel. The Messiah has come," another cried.

Deborah caught her breath. The Messiah. How many years

had they prayed for his birth? How long had Israel waited for deliverance? *Can it be true that the long-desired one has arrived? And in our stable?*

As the shepherds left, talking excitedly among themselves at the wonders of this night, she crept inside to where she could see the newborn baby lying on a bed of straw in the stone manger, where the animals fed on less momentous occasions.

Her heart pounded in her chest, and she could not breathe. Surely the shepherds were drunk. Or she had misunderstood them. Surely nothing as wonderful as the coming of the Messiah could ever touch her life. Yet he was coming. The prophets had foretold it. What if the shepherds' words were true? *Oh, Yahweh, if only it could be true!*

She saw Mary motioning to her. "Come see him," she invited, smiling. Deborah handed the things she had brought to Joseph, and hesitantly approached the manger where the baby lay.

"He's beautiful," she breathed, bending over to get a closer look in the flickering light. The baby opened his eyes and looked straight into hers. She felt the jolt as his gaze connected with hers. Never had anyone looked at her that way. It was as though this tiny baby could see straight through her into her soul. She could feel a cool balm spreading over her wounds and scars, a warmth filling all her empty spaces.

Suddenly, she was on her knees in the straw, her gaze still glued to his, tears spilling down her face. *"Eli,"* she whispered. "My God."

"His name will be *Yeshua,*" Mary said. "It means *Savior,* one who will save his people from their sins."

The baby seemed to smile, then closed his eyes, breaking the connection. Still, she was powerless to rise. She bent over, much as she had seen Mary do in labor, and sobbed into her hands, letting her loneliness, her despair wash away with the tears.

Deborah didn't understand what had happened. She only knew she was no longer invisible. *Yeshua* had looked into the deepest part of her worthless being and loved her anyway. Never again would she doubt that she was real. Never again would she be empty or alone.

"Once you are *Real,*" the Skin Horse told the Velveteen Rabbit, "you can't become unreal again. It lasts for always."

LYDIA

THEME: *Provision*

Scripture: Acts 16:13–15, 40

*S*ighing, Lydia picked up the basket containing her lunch and began the short walk to the market square. The time of mourning for her husband was finished. It was time for her to get on with life. *Whether or not I want to,* she thought. Without Marcus everything seemed meaningless.

When she had dressed up in the evenings and taken so much time arranging her hair, it had been to see the admiration in Marcus' eyes. When she had planned a special menu with the cook or prepared some delicacy, it had been to watch him eat with enjoyment. When she had redecorated a room or added a treasure she had found in the market, her satisfaction was not complete until he had expressed delight in it.

Worst of all, she had no one to talk with about anything that really mattered. Of course, she loved her three children deeply, but Decimus and Augustus were boys, and Claudia was too young to understand. Who would share her search for a god she could trust? Who would listen to her dreams or reach out in the night to hold her when she had a nightmare? It was as though her once-colorful life had been painted over in tones of black and gray.

At the edge of the square she stopped, looking down the flat, broad stones of the *Via Egnatia* that led to *Neapolis* on the Aegean Sea nearly ten miles distant. She turned and looked behind the white stone colonnade, beyond the sun-bleached shops to where that same road disappeared into the western hills toward Rome, across the Adriatic Sea. *It is true, as they say, that all roads lead to Rome, eventually.*

She never had been to Rome, though Marcus had made the journey several times to deliver his wares to the household of the emperor. The purple of the beautiful cloth Marcus provided did not come from the unstable dyes produced from roots. It came only from the shell of the murex, an ocean mollusk found in the Great Sea [the Mediterranean] and in the Aegean that emptied into it. His cloth was coveted by those who wore the purple to proclaim their wealth and position.

Marcus had prospered as a seller of purple. The white stone house he had built them at the edge of Philippi was large and comfortable, and she had many slaves to see that the household ran smoothly. She and her children would not want for material goods.

She sighed again. She had great wealth, but it did not satisfy. *What my children and I want, what we need, is a husband and father.*

How she missed his strength, his wisdom now as she prepared to carry on the business he had left behind when he dropped dead in the street on his way home from the shop one evening.

She had not worked in the business in years. She was afraid she had forgotten anything she ever had known about the making of purple dye and cloth, though her parents had been sellers of purple back in Thyatira. Lydia had been a young bride when they died. Shortly thereafter, her husband had moved the business a hundred miles to Philippi, a Roman colony and the largest city in Macedonia.

The decree of Caesar Augustus that Roman families relocate in the colonies to make them easier to govern had brought many to Philippi who were entitled to wear the royal purple. In addition the officers from the nearby garrison were encouraged to make their retirement homes here.

Marcus had preferred that she stay at home, run their household, and rear their children. He had used slaves in the manufacture of the dye and the forming of the cloth. Over them he had appointed Caleb, an elderly Jewish man with years of experience in making cloth, as overseer. She would have to lean heavily on Caleb's wisdom in the days ahead.

Most Romans shared the Emperor Claudius' disdain for Jews that had led him to expel all of them from Rome. There weren't many Jews in Philippi, not even enough to form the *minion* of ten men required by their religion to establish a synagogue.

Lately, she had been walking the mile and a half to the bank of the Gangites River to join a group of Jewish women who worshipped their unseen God there each week. *Yahweh,* they called him. She was not a Jew, but the high moral standards of the Jewish law and the love expressed in the teachings of *Yahweh* appealed to her, far more than those of the cruel, hedonistic Roman gods.

Caleb and I will have no problems over his religion, she thought, *but how will he feel about a woman running a business, about obeying her orders?* Of course, women had more freedom here in the modern city of Philippi than they did in many places. She knew a few who had their own businesses.

As she neared the shop, she could see that Caleb had already raised the awnings and had displayed samples of their goods attractively on a small table. Behind the table and two stools, the doorway to the main shop was open.

From the work area behind the shop, she could hear muted voices in several strange tongues. Some of the slaves had been with Marcus from the beginning and had become expert at weaving and dying the soft wools and crisp linens, as well as processing the silks they imported from the Far East.

"*Boker tov,* mistress," Caleb greeted her, his brown eyes twinkling in his swarthy, wrinkled face. "What can I do for you this morning?"

Apprehension slid over her. Caleb was not acknowledging the fact that she had come to run the shop. "Good morning, Caleb," she replied. "I am so glad you are here. I will need your expert advice if I am to learn to run this business."

The old man's eyes narrowed as he stroked his thick, gray beard. "Perhaps I misunderstood, mistress, but I thought your eldest son, Decimus, would assume the role of proprietor. He has spent hours here with his father—*zal* [may he rest in peace]—and though he has much to learn, he is a bright boy and soon will be of age."

Lydia knew Decimus hated the purple business. Soon after his father's death, he had expressed the wish to buy an officership in the army as soon as he was old enough. She would not try to force him to give up his dreams.

It was thirteen-year-old Augustus who had loved going to the shop with his father. He would come home talking of nothing but the fascinating process of extracting the dye from the murex shells and the different methods of dying various kinds of cloth. Of course, he still was too young to take his father's place as head of the business.

"Caleb," she said firmly, laying her hand on his shoulder, "I will be running the business, with, I hope, your invaluable help. You will have a position here as long as you want it. Decimus is only fifteen. Someday, he—or perhaps Augustus—will take over here, but meanwhile I must run this business or sell it."

The old man dropped his gaze. "Yes, mistress," he replied stiffly.

Oh, Caleb, she thought, *please don't give me trouble because of your old-fashioned ideas that a woman is good for nothing but to bear children, cook, and clean, and wait upon her man. I have done all that, and I loved those precious, pleasant days at home, but things are different now that Marcus is gone.*

"One never knows, Caleb," she said, unable to resist needling him a little, "it may be my daughter, Claudia, who becomes the next seller of purple in our family. Of course, she is only ten and would need to grow up a bit more."

Caleb gasped. "Oh, mistress, I ..."

"Caleb," she interrupted, "I would prefer that Marcus were still here to take his place in this man's world and let me continue my role as homemaker, mother, and wife. But he is not, and I have no choice but to try to fill his sandals, at least until Decimus or Augustus—or Claudia—is of age and shows an interest in the business. I don't plan to sell. I want the business to pass to one of them."

The old man stared at her, then again dropped his gaze. She hoped he could not hear the frantic beating of her heart at the thought that he might decide to leave, to take that much-earned retirement Marcus had told her he was anticipating. He was not a slave, and she could not force him to stay.

"You have been a faithful employee of my husband," she added persuasively, "and I need you to continue to serve me in that same manner, Caleb, to teach me all you can. May I depend upon your help?"

Caleb lifted his eyes to hers. His manner still was stiff, but he bowed his head in acknowledgment of what she had said. "I understand, mistress. I will let you know," he promised and moved into the shop where she heard him giving orders to someone in the workroom.

She heard the clank of metal and looked across the table straight into the piercing blue eyes of a Roman centurion.

"I seek Marcus, the seller of purple," he demanded. "I have come from Rome with orders from the emperor."

"My husband is recently deceased, sir," she responded, "but I will be happy to fill your orders."

His fierce eyes studied her for a moment. "Very well," he conceded. "This is what I require." He rattled off a huge order that Lydia was unable to recall after the fifth or sixth item. "I will need it by the end of next week, as I must make the last sailing for Rome before the storms begin."

Lydia took a deep breath. She had no idea how long it would take to put together such an order, but she was unwilling to admit to this stranger how inexperienced she was.

"Sir, if you will kindly repeat your order slowly so that I may write it down, I will have it ready for you by the end of next week," she promised rashly. She prayed she could fulfill the promise. To successfully complete the order would establish her as a worthy successor to her husband as the emperor's supplier of purple cloth. To fail could ruin her.

Surely Caleb would be able to meet the centurion's demands, if he decided to stay and work with her. Fear tightened its iron band around her heart at the thought that he might leave. There was no way she could fill this order, much less run the business without him.

"*Yahweh,*" she prayed desperately, "I am so alone. If you really do exist, if you really can hear my prayer, please don't let Caleb leave me."

GRACE

I knew the fifty-two-year-old widow, whom I will call Grace, was having a hard time dealing with the loss of her husband, who died during surgery following a massive heart attack. She had married Carl when she was sixteen and had spent her life as his wife— making his home pleasant and comfortable, raising his children, loving him.

Now, though she never had worked outside the home, she knew she would have to find a paying job. Carl's last medical bills and funeral expenses had depleted all their savings, as well as his life insurance. The pittance she would draw from his Social Security would be far short of her needs, even if she were frugal.

She shuddered at the thought of living with any of her grown children, she confided, much as she loved them and their children. She didn't want to intrude into their lives, and she wanted her own space. She wanted to stay in the home she and Carl had shared for thirty-six years.

Her home was paid for, thank God, though she did not know how she could come up with the money for insurance and property taxes. "I simply have to find a job." she told me on the phone when I called to check on her one morning. "I'm relatively able-bodied, except for some arthritis in my joints and a little high blood pressure, nothing that would prevent me from holding a job," she said. "The problem is: I am fifty-two years old, and I have no marketable skills. What on earth can I do to support myself?"

I prayed with her and promised to let her know if I heard of a job she could do. It was as we hung up, she said later, that she realized it wasn't just the money. It was the loneliness, her aching loneliness for Carl, the emptiness of her days and nights.

She had slept in the last pajama jacket he had worn until she had to give in and wash it. She knew she would have to go through his clothes soon and give them to someone who could use them, but she just couldn't bring herself to cut that last tie with him.

The empty, lonely years stretched bleakly ahead of her, and suddenly she was angry. "I am so angry at you, Carl, for going off and leaving me," she cried aloud. Then she felt ashamed of her selfish words. She knew he would not have gone if he had had a choice. Well, maybe he would have at the last when he was so sick. Maybe dying seemed the lesser of the evils he faced.

Oh, God, she cried desperately, *I loved him so. What on earth am I going to do without him?*

A LITTLE PRINCESS

Sara Crewe, the protagonist in Frances Hodgson Burnett's novel, *A Little Princess*, was treated like a princess, so long as money came in to the exclusive boarding school where her widowed father had left her while he went away to war. Then the flow of support stopped, and Sara was given the sad news that her father had been killed.

The school's headmistress decided to keep the orphaned girl, but as a servant. She sent her to live in the unheated attic and provided her the poorest of food. Sara's heart ached for her beloved father, as she realized that there was no one left in the world who really cared about her.

At least two of the many movie and TV versions of the story end with the eventual discovery of Sara's father recuperating in a hospital, they are reunited and all is well. In Burnett's original story, Captain Crewe truly is dead, but Sara finally is located by her father's former partner and inherits a great sum of money. She goes to live with the partner, and never again is subjected to the sadistic care of the headmistress.

In either version Sara's loving father provides for her, just as our heavenly Father provides for widows and orphans. David said in Psalm 146:9, "The Lord watches over the alien and sustains the fatherless and the widow." Likewise, in Deuteronomy 10:18, Moses wrote: "He defends the cause of the fatherless and the widow."

UNDERSTANDING LYDIA

Little is told about Lydia in the story in Acts 16, which is believed to have taken place around AD 50. We learn that she was a business woman, that this lady with the Roman name met with a group of Jewish women on the riverbank to worship the God of the Jews, that she was well-off financially, that she had a household of slaves and probably family, that she had a house large enough to accommodate Paul and his companions, and that she became Paul's first convert to Christianity in Europe.

For more than that we must read between the lines. Why was she running a business when she had a household to run? Either she had never married or she was a widow, carrying on the business her husband had established. Most historians accept the latter.

The size of her house and household indicates that she was wealthy, as would be expected of a seller of purple, who would have realized a good profit from the sale of this rare, expensive commodity.

Apparently, she was a respected leader whose home automatically became the meeting place of those who joined in her newfound faith. Even before then, since she is the only one of the woman worshippers named, it is possible she was a leader of the group.

Lydia was not a destitute widow in need of the basic necessities of life—food, clothing, medicine, housing. Her needs were more subtle. She needed assistance in running a business in a man's world. She needed strength and support in managing many slaves or servants, both in the business and in her home. She desperately needed something to live for now that the man around whom she had built her life was gone.

Lydia found what many modern-day widows have discovered when they cry out in despair: "The eternal God is your refuge, and underneath are the everlasting arms" (Deut. 33:27).

GOD AND WIDOWS

God has a special place in his heart for the widow. He even promises to be her husband. "In that day," the Lord says, "you will call me 'my husband'; you will no longer call me 'my master'"(Hos. 2:16). And also, "For your Maker is your husband—the Lord Almighty is his name" (Isa. 54:5).

In Exodus 22:22–24, God warns severely, "Do not take advantage of a widow or an orphan. If you do and they cry out to me, I will certainly hear their cry. My anger will be aroused, and I will kill you with the sword; your wives will become widows and your children fatherless."

Wow. Is there anybody else in the Bible to whom God has made such a promise? In addition, there are notable stories in the Old Testament to support the claims that God always is looking out for widows.

THE WIDOW AT ZAREPHATH

In 1 Kings 17:7–24, we are told that after the ravens stopped feeding Elijah as he hid from wicked Queen Jezebel, God told him to go to Zarephath, for he had prepared for a widow there to feed him. When Elijah arrived, he met a woman gathering firewood and asked her to bring him a drink of water and a piece of bread. She told him that she had only enough flour and oil to make one small cake of bread, which she had planned to bake for her son and herself to eat as a last meal before they died of starvation.

Elijah told her to make some bread for him first and promised that her oil and flour would not run out until God again sent rain on the land to replenish its grain and olive oil. She obeyed, and found that what Elijah spoke was true.

Later this same widow's son died and Elijah, through the power of the Lord, raised him from the dead. God was looking out for this widow.

THE WIDOW AND THE OIL

In an account from 2 Kings 4:1–7, another widow, the wife of a man from the company of the prophets, came to Elisha for help when her creditors were about to sell her two sons as slaves to pay her debts. Elisha told her to borrow all the vessels she could from her neighbors and begin to pour from her small cruse of oil until they all were filled. The oil lasted until the last vessel was filled, and Elisha told her to go and sell the oil, pay her debts, and live on what was left.

I've often wondered if the widow had been able to come up with more vessels, would the oil have continued to flow? It is likely, for the oil only stopped flowing when she ran out of something to hold it. God took care of this widow, too, but did she limit his blessings because her faith wasn't big enough to hold them?

HAGAR

Hagar was not a widow, but she might as well have been. When Sarah forced Abraham to banish her and her son, Ishmael, into the desert, Hagar had no husband, no one to protect or sustain her. Genesis 21:8–20 tells us that once the skin of water Abraham had provided was exhausted, she placed the young boy under the shade of a bush and went a few feet away so she wouldn't have to watch him die.

God had other plans, though. He came to Hagar's rescue when she had nowhere else to turn. He heard her son crying and provided a well of water that saved his life and hers.

Hagar's son lived 137 years, according to Genesis 25:17. He married an Egyptian woman, like his mother, and produced twelve sons who became the rulers of twelve tribes of a great nation, just as God had promised Abraham in Genesis 21:13 and Hagar in Genesis 21:18. God was looking out for Hagar.

However, as Rebekah and Jacob learned, "God cannot be mocked. A man reaps what he sows" (Gal. 6:7). The bungling attempt of Abraham and Sarah to "help" God fulfill his promise set the stage for violent hostility from Ishmael's descendants, the Arabs, toward Isaac's descendants, the Israelis, that continues to this day.

RUTH AND NAOMI

On a happier note we have the familiar story of two widows from the little book of Ruth. Naomi and her daughter-in-law Ruth both had suffered widowhood in the land of Moab, where Naomi and her husband and sons had gone to escape a famine in Israel. After her husband and both sons died, Naomi decided to return to her homeland, and Ruth insisted on going with her. You know the story of how God provided for them through the kindness of Boaz, Naomi's next of kin. (See Ruth 2—4.)

Part of Ruth's loyalty was to Naomi, but part of it was to the God whom Naomi had introduced to her. "Your people will be my people and your God my God," she vowed in Ruth 1:16. As a result of that commitment, Ruth became the mother of Jesse, the grandmother of David, and, ultimately, the ancestor of *Yeshua haMeshiach,* Jesus the Messiah. Could any widow have been more blessed?

GOD STILL LOVES WIDOWS

The New Testament, too, shows us that, just as God has his eye on the sparrow, he has his eye on the widow.

Jesus was watching when the poor widow tossed all that she had into the offering, and he gave her a lasting memorial (Luke 21:1–4). He was watching when the widow of Nain was burying her son, and he gave him back to her (Luke 7:11–15). He saw his widowed mother grieving at the foot of the cross and made provision for her (John 19:25–27).

Stories abound of widows in our own time who have had their needs for life's necessities met in miraculous ways through

200 / TIMELESS needs, ETERNAL

their trust in the Lord. For example, as Grace was praying desperately for a job, my boss came to me asking if I knew anyone who could help us out for a few days. The job was one that required no special skills, and instantly, I thought of Grace. Coincidence? Hardly. The Holy Spirit obviously was at work on her behalf.

Grace eagerly accepted the job, which grew into a full-time, permanent position. Interacting with coworkers helped her become involved with the needs of others and freed her from dwelling on her own troubles. Her empty days were filled, her financial needs were met, and she discovered she had skills of which she had not been aware. She became a valued employee of that office until her retirement. God was looking out for Grace.

James 1:27 says, "Religion that God our Father accepts as pure and faultless is this: to look after orphans and widows in their distress." In addition, there are many passages that apply to all Christians, but certainly include the widow, as well.

> "So do not worry, saying 'What shall we eat?' or 'What shall we drink?' or 'What shall we wear?' … your heavenly Father knows that you need them. But seek first his kingdom and his righteousness, and all these things will be given to you as well." (Matt. 6:31–33)

> "Do not be anxious about anything, but in everything, by prayer and petition, with thanksgiving, present your requests to God." (Phil. 4:6)

"Even if my father and mother abandon me, the Lord will hold me close." (Ps. 27:10 NLT)

"I can do everything through him who gives me strength." (Phil. 4:13)

"You, Lord, give true peace to those who depend on you, because they trust you." (Isa. 26:3 NCV)

THE PEACE THAT PASSES UNDERSTANDING

For a widow who had a loving spouse, like Grace, there will always be moments when a desperate longing for her mate sweeps over her, when her loneliness penetrates the marrow of her bones, when she wants that missing companionship more than she wants daily food, when she despairs of the bleakness of her circumstances.

Thank God, however, that our peace and our joy do not depend upon circumstances. As one widow commented, "When I get those moments of excruciating loneliness—and believe me, there are times—I just begin to talk to God, and he fills all the holes with his presence."

I learned something about this unfathomable, hole-filling peace myself when our daughter announced she was going to marry a young man my husband and I could see was a scoundrel. We were told he had bragged to his friends that his "conversion" and baptism in our church had been only to convince us to let him date our daughter. She, of course, could see nothing beyond the stars in her eyes.

Devastated at what our daughter's life was sure to be like with him, I called a special friend to fast and pray with me. One morning, as I wept before the Lord, I heard him answer. No, there was no audible voice, but the words spread through my mind, "Trust me. It will be all right."

"How can it be all right?" I argued. "Once she marries him, she will be stuck with him for life."

"Trust me," he repeated.

Somehow I did, as the marriage plans progressed and the wedding took place. Circumstances looked bleak as the newlyweds left on their honeymoon, I learned, however, that my peace did not depend upon circumstances, but upon the promises of God.

Three rocky years later, our daughter was free. The young man had repeatedly broken his marriage vows, beginning about a week after the honeymoon, giving her a biblical reason to leave him and start a new life.

BACK TO LYDIA

Lydia picked up her lunch basket and carried it to the small garden behind the shop. Through the doorway she could see Caleb giving orders to a slave, waving his hands commandingly.

She had apologized to the old man for her reckless promise to the centurion, but Caleb was still a little huffy about the burden she had placed on all of them. He had come through with the order, though, just in time. The bundles of precious purple-trimmed cloth were wrapped protectively in cheaper material and waiting in the shop for the centurion to pick up today.

She hoped he would come early this afternoon. Today was *Yom Shishi,* and the Jewish *Shabbat* would begin with the appearance of the first star in the evening sky. She wanted to close the shop early. She knew Caleb would want to prepare, and her own pulse quickened as she anticipated joining the women on the riverbank for the service this evening.

How she loved the rituals of *Shabbat*—the lighting of the candles, the *challah* bread, the sweet fruit of the vine, the simple prayers that recognized the goodness of *Yahweh.* She had been chosen to say the prayer over the ceremonial wine tonight.

"Baruch atta, Adonai, Elohanu, melek ha-olam, borey p'ri hagafen," she practiced the unfamiliar Hebrew words. *Or is it* "hagufin"? she wondered uncertainly. "Blessed are you, O Lord, our God, king of the universe, creator of the fruit of the vine," she translated.

"You are becoming very Jewish, mistress," Caleb said softly from behind her. Lydia felt her face flush with embarrassment. She hadn't meant for anyone to hear her.

"How I wish my husband could have known your *Yahweh,* Caleb," she said wistfully. "He had little time for the cruel, hedonistic Roman gods. He would have loved the God of Abraham, Isaac, and Jacob." She sighed. "But I didn't know him myself until after Marcus died."

She hesitated, then plunged on, "Where do you think Marcus is now, Caleb? Will *Yahweh* forgive him for not knowing when he really did not have a chance? Or is he condemned to some place of torment forever?"

The old man cleared his throat uneasily. "He did not know of the yearly sacrifices to roll his sins forward until *haMeshiach* comes," he said. "He was a good man. We will just have to leave him in the hands of his Creator, mistress."

Lydia knew by the way his eyes did not meet hers that Caleb had little hope for Marcus in the afterlife.

"Caleb, have you heard what those visitors in town are saying about the Messiah?" she questioned. "They joined our group of women on the riverbank last *Shabbat,* and all they talked about was this *Yeshua* who was crucified in Jerusalem some time ago. They say he arose from the dead, that he is the Son of God, the Messiah who has come to save us all from our sins."

Caleb spit on the ground. "Blasphemy!" he said vehemently, his dark eyes flashing. "May *haShem* strike them with lightning from above!"

She did not wish to argue with him, but there was a longing in her soul to believe what the little man from Tarsus and his friends had said. She couldn't wait to get back there this evening and hear more about it. The men had promised to be there.

Lydia was the last to arrive. The centurion had not come for his order until the day was over. She had sent Caleb home earlier so he could prepare for *Shabbat* with his family. When the centurion finally arrived and the transaction was complete, she had gathered her shawl and her basket and hurried west of the city to the riverbank.

The first star shone brightly in the sky, and the short, stocky Jew called Paul was speaking. "Daughters of Abraham," he said, then seeing Lydia join them, he added, "and you God-fearing Gentiles, it is to us that the message of salvation has been sent."

Lydia listened avidly to Paul's story of how God's son had become *Emmanuel,* God with us, through his birth to a virgin in the little town of Bethlehem, as he said had been foretold by the Jewish prophets. She absorbed the stories of his sinless life, his miracles. Then as Paul told of his rejection by the Jewish leaders, his crucifixion, his burial in a borrowed tomb, her heart began to pound. Her head felt light, as though she were about to faint, something she had not done since her last pregnancy nearly eleven years ago.

Paul's voice was firm and sure as he finished, "But God raised him from the dead, and for many days he was seen by those who had traveled with him from Galilee to Jerusalem. He has conquered both sin and death, beloved, and set us free."

She felt Paul's keen eyes upon her. He came over and took her hands as she fell to her knees, tears streaming unheeded down her face. "Do you believe, sister?" he asked.

She nodded her head, unable to speak. Then the words poured out of her, as Paul guided her in accepting *Yeshua haMeshiach* as her

Savior and Lord. She was unaware of others around her who also were falling to their knees and praying with Luke and others to ask the Savior to be their Lord.

A deep peace flowed over Lydia like warm anointing oil, easing her hurts, filling her lonely spaces.

※

For an idea of what Paul might have said there on the riverbank at Philippi, we must go to Acts 13:13–48, since his words to the Philippian Jews and Lydia are not recorded. However, Acts 16:14b says, "The Lord opened her heart to respond to Paul's message."

That Lydia was sincere is obvious from the fact that she led her entire household in baptism, and insisted Paul and his companions enjoy the hospitality of her home for the remainder of their stay in Philippi. It was on their way from Lydia's house to the riverbank on another occasion that Paul cast the demon out of the slave girl, an act that led to his and Silas's imprisonment and miraculous release (Acts 16:16-40).

Lydia's home became the meeting place of the new Christians in Philippi, to whom Paul wrote the Philippian letter some eleven or twelve years later from his prison cell in Rome.

Perhaps because she had chosen to worship the one true God instead of the decadent gods of the Romans around her, God supplied all Lydia's needs. In addition he gave her the opportunity to hear the gospel and accept Jesus as her personal Savior. He also gave her a memorial in the New Testament.

God was looking out for Lydia, Hagar, Ruth, Naomi, the widow of Zarephath, the prophet's widow, and Grace. Can we doubt that he will do the same for any desperate widow today who sincerely seeks him?

10

MARY

THEME: *Submission*

Scripture: Matthew 1–2; Luke 2

*M*ary stood watching until Jesus disappeared over the horizon. He had said he was going to see his cousin, who was baptizing people in the River Jordan. She didn't know why he suddenly wanted to see John, but he had been restless and preoccupied lately.

She sighed. Her eldest son always had been different—from the night of his birth in that stable in Bethlehem all through his growing up years. Once, when he was twelve, he had disappeared as they were leaving Jerusalem after the *Pesach* sacrifices. They had found him in the temple talking with the elders, amazing them with his knowledge of the Scriptures.

When she had scolded him for frightening them, he had given

her the strangest look and said the oddest thing: "Did you not know that I must be about my Father's business?" he had asked, his compelling eyes holding hers.

Mary had felt a chill slide down her spine. She knew he had special work to do. From the time the angel Gabriel had told her she would bear the Son of the Most High, she had known her first-born would be no ordinary child. She knew he was destined to save his people from their sins. She did not understand how that would happen, but she knew it would have to be extraordinary.

As Jesus grew, she had told him all the wondrous things that had been told her—by the angel, by the shepherds and the magi, by the prophetess Anna, by old Simeon at the temple. He seemed to have no problem understanding those things. She had pondered them in her heart for years and still did not quite know what to make of them.

Nor did she know what to make of this sudden departure to visit John. The carpenter's shop was busy right now. Of course, Jesus had trained his two closest brothers well in the craft these last few years. Simon loved working with wood and became almost as skilled at it as Jesus himself, but she knew James preferred his studies with the Rabbi to making tools and furniture. His heart just wasn't in it. Neither was Jesus' anymore. He had loved working in the shop with Joseph. Once, he told her how he enjoyed the pungent smell of the wood as his saw cut through it, the satiny feel of smooth-planed wood against his palm.

Now, she sometimes found him standing at the workbench with a piece of wood forgotten in his hands, his eyes focused on something she could not see, unaware of her presence. Then he would come back to her for a time, teasing her, presenting her with something he had made for her with his gifted hands.

Sometimes, looking at his hands, she felt fear. She didn't know why. She wasn't given to fear. She had known fear only briefly when the angel Gabriel had appeared to her that day some thirty years ago. Then her fear had been swallowed up by the wonder of what he was telling her.

"Do not be afraid, Mary, you have found favor with God," the angel had said. "You will be with child and give birth to a son, and you are to give him the name Jesus."

When she had questioned how this could be, since she was a virgin, he had answered, "The Holy Spirit will come upon you, and the power of the Most High will overshadow you. So the holy one to be born will be called the Son of God."

Even knowing her neighbors, her family, and probably even Joseph likely would believe she had slept with a man outside of marriage had not caused her to fear. She had felt only a humble gratitude that the Most High had chosen her from among all the Jewish women of all time to bear his Son, Jesus. *Yeshua.* The Hebrew name meant *Savior.* She was to be the mother of *haMeshiach,* the Messiah promised to Israel all these many years.

She had not even known fear when she knew her baby was about to be born and there was no room for them in the inn. She had felt the weight of destiny upon her, as she struggled with the birth pangs, but then she had known only joy as she laid her newborn son in the straw-filled manger. She had felt the glory of the Lord around her as the star shone above and the awestruck shepherds crowded into the cave to see the one of whom the angels had spoken.

She had not known fear when her other children were born here in Nazareth, with her mother and the midwife to help her. She had not known fear as she reared them, even in the years after Joseph's death when she had faced that formidable task alone.

Now, for the first time, she knew fear. The weight of his destiny was upon Jesus. She could sense it, for she always had felt a special bond with him. Sometimes he had seemed like any other child, and she had mothered him much as she had her later children. She had nourished him, doctored his skinned knees, comforted his tears, and watched him play in the dirt with little wooden toys Joseph made for him. She had heard him recite perfectly the words of his *bar mitzvah,* and watched him perfect his carpenter's skills.

The people of Nazareth thought he was nothing more than a carpenter, the son of Mary and Joseph who had grown up playing with their own sons. Their daughters had cast hopeful eyes upon him, then moved on to more receptive candidates.

Yet Mary knew Jesus was more than that. He was the son of the Most High. She had merely been the vessel by which the Savior had come into the world. She shivered in the heat of the day with the dread of what terrible thing might be required of her beloved firstborn son. To be the Savior of the world surely would require some awesome deed.

She had questioned Jesus about the Scriptures that spoke of *haMeshiach,* and he quoted to her from Isaiah about the virgin bearing a son, and from Jonah about him being born in Bethlehem. True to the prophecies, he had been born of a virgin in Bethlehem, but Mary knew there was more to it than those gentle words. She had heard the Rabbi read the words of the prophet Isaiah concerning *haMeshiach:*

> "He was despised and rejected by men, a man of sorrows, and familiar with suffering…. He was pierced for our transgressions, he was crushed for our iniquities; the punishment that brought us peace was upon him, and by his wounds we are healed." (Isa. 53:3, 5)

She shuddered and tried to push the painful words away, but they haunted her, especially now that Jesus was pulling away, reaching out for something she did not understand. The terrifying words of Isaiah invaded her thoughts again. *Sorrows, suffering, wounds.* "Oh, *Yahweh,*" she cried desperately, "what sacrifice will he be called upon to make? How soon will it come? Will he be able to bear it? Will I?"

DONNA

We had prayed her son Todd safely out of Iraq once. Then, my friend, whom I will call Donna, e-mailed me asking for prayer again. The young Marine was being sent back for another tour of duty. He had been home for a brief visit, and she was taking him this morning to catch his plane.

I felt for her. Though I'm not afraid to fly, just putting one of my children on a plane to anywhere always leaves me shaken. I hate watching that small speck fly off into the clouds, so vulnerable to storms, to mechanical failure, to accident, carrying my child farther and farther away.

I knew it was worse for Donna, knowing that, provided his plane arrived safely at its destination, he would face even more danger in a place where war raged and terrorists threatened. I realized it was cowardly of me, but I was glad I wasn't there to witness their goodbyes.

Donna pushed the thought of Todd's eminent departure away, concentrating on his perfectly creased uniform, the impeccably polished boots, the cap sitting on his blond head at a jaunty angle. *How handsome he is.*

"You won't be allowed to go any farther, Mom," Todd warned. "You know how tight airport security is now."

"I know, son," she answered, drinking in the affection she saw in his blue eyes, knowing that, at best, it would have to last her for a long time, or at worst, forever.

Todd put his arm around her and hugged her to him. "I love you, Mom," he said, a catch in his voice. "Thanks for always being there for me, even when I didn't want it," he finished, with a chuckle.

She couldn't answer. She swallowed the lump in her throat and fought back the tears threatening to overflow.

He gave her a little shake. "Don't worry, Mom. I'll be okay. Just pray for me. I've always said, 'Nobody can get through to God like my Mom.'"

She laughed shakily. "Every day, son. Know that you will be prayed for many times every day." *And throughout the long nights,* she added silently, *when I hear the terrible news from over there and wonder if you were one of those blown up or shot.*

"Flight 744 now boarding at Gate 2," the loudspeakers blared, and her heart skipped as she turned back to him in wordless anguish. There was nothing more to be said.

He hugged her again, gave her a quick kiss on the cheek, and let her go. "'Bye. I promise to write or call." Then he was running down the long hallway, turning once to wave.

Donna waved back and stood watching until he disappeared through the last set of doors. Then she turned and walked slowly back to the rows of seats in front of a wall of windows where she would be able to see the plane ascend once it had circled the airport.

She took a tissue from her pocket and dabbed futilely at the tears that flooded her eyes and spilled down her cheeks as the plane came in sight around the corner of the building and taxied down the runway. As it lifted effortlessly, circling higher and higher into the sky, she felt her heart contract.

No longer caring about the people around her, she gave up trying to wipe the tears away and just let them fall. Sobs from the depth of her being shuddered through her body.

My precious son, the fruit of my body, the love of my soul, is on that tiny speck up there in the clouds. The thought left her without the strength to stand, and she sank into the seat behind her.

Todd had wanted to go. Nothing she had said could dissuade him. He wanted to fight for his country, he said, to do his part.

"Freedom does not come cheap, Mom," he had said. "Every generation has had to pay with its blood for the freedom we have enjoyed here in America. It's my turn, and likely I'll come home safe and sound when it's over. Dad flew countless dangerous missions in Vietnam," he reminded her, "and he came home with just that small limp."

"And some horrible memories that haunted him until the day he died, Todd," she had said. But, much as she dreaded for him to go, she knew he was right. She could not deny that she was proud of him for his courage and patriotism.

If only he had made that commitment to the Lord before he went, she agonized. *If something should happen to him—God forbid—at least I would have the assurance that I would see him again in heaven.*

"I'm not ready for that, Mom," he had told her. "I suspect that someday I will commit my life to him, but I have to know it is real, and not just something I'm doing because you and Dad had me in church every time the doors opened as I was growing up."

Fear traveled down Donna's spine. What if Todd got killed over there in the Middle East? What if that plane he was on right now crashed? He would be lost for eternity.

"Oh, God, please," she whispered desperately, walking away from the window that now showed only empty sky. "Place a hedge of protection around my son. Send someone across his path who can reach him with your truth. Don't let him go into eternity without you."

THE UGLY DUCKLING

Mother Duck loved all her ducklings, but she had to admit that the big one was strange looking. Some even said he was ugly. "Hideously ugly" was the Gray Goose's comment.

Poor thing. On land he's gawky and awkward, but once he gets into the water, he glides across the pond like a dragonfly skimming the surface. It's a shame he can't just stay in the water.

She supposed he was somewhat ugly, tall and gangly, the opposite of his cute, fluffy little brothers and sisters. She would never say so, though. The pitiful creature had enough to bear without hearing his own mother put him down.

However, as time passed and her outsized child just grew bigger and more awkward looking, she could see that he was unhappy in the barnyard with all the other fowl. She could sense his pain at their cruel mockery. She was not surprised and didn't even protest when he decided to go off on his own.

She was a little ashamed of the relief she felt as she watched him waddle across the field and out of sight over the hill. She knew she would never forget him, and she wished him well, but he obviously did not belong here.

Mother Duck probably never knew that this pitiful creature

she had somehow hatched, that walked like a duck and swam like a duck, wasn't a duck. He was an elegant white swan, full of grace and beauty that far surpassed the ordinary barnyard fowl who had scorned him. He was different because of who he was, and what he was destined to become.

UNDERSTANDING MARY

No matter what he looked like physically, there was nothing ugly about Jesus. He was the creator of beauty. Still, like the mother of the Ugly Duckling, Mary must have thought her eldest son was different from his brothers and sisters. And her memory often must have whispered to her of the miraculous happenings of his birth and growing-up years.

Every Jewish maiden since the nation had existed must have wondered at some time if she would be the one God would choose to bring the Messiah into the world. When Gabriel brought Mary the announcement that she would be the one, other than to ask how this could happen to a virgin, she didn't question it.

Unlike the Innkeeper's Wife, Mary's humble nature did not spring from low self-esteem. She appears to have possessed a nature wholly attuned to God, and wholly willing to do whatever he asked of her. She was "the servant of the Lord" and, as such, she humbly accepted the role he had chosen for her to play.

That Mary had a gentle influence upon Jesus is evident from

their interaction at the wedding in Cana recorded in John 2:1–11. Concerned that their hosts were about to be disgraced by running out of wine before the celebration was over, and confident that he could do something about it, she told Jesus of their plight.

When Jesus fondly chided her, "Dear woman, why do you involve me? My time has not yet come," Mary was not in the least perturbed. She instructed the servants to do whatever he asked of them. And, to please his mother, the Creator of the vine changed ordinary water into the finest wine and saved the reputation of their hosts.

It is said that Adolf Hitler's mother influenced him to explore the occult and encouraged him to despise the Jews. We all know the results of that mother's influence. Hitler became deeply involved in the black arts, and he annihilated millions of Jews, as well as other people. He went to his death believing he would rule the world as the antichrist.

Conversely, God knew exactly what he was doing when he chose lovely young Mary to be the mother of his Son. She was just the kind of person he wanted to influence the human side of Jesus in his early, formative years.

REBEL AT HEART

All of us have inherited old Mother Eve's rebellious nature, some more than others. I used to wonder why my children seemed to have received more than their fair share, until one day I took a long, hard look at their mother.

I don't want to be a rebel. I really don't. I want to obey gracefully and humbly like Mary when God tells me to do something. Still, it is the battle I find myself fighting more than any other. Paul would understand that. "I do not do the good things I want to do, but I do the bad things I do not want to do" he mourned in Romans 7:19 (NCV).

Apparently, unlike Paul and me, it never occurred to Mary to rebel. In nearly all we read about her, we see that she accepted whatever role the Lord assigned her.

Can you imagine her hurt as she saw Jesus dragged through the streets like a common criminal? Can you feel her pain as she watched the cat-o'-nine-tails rip the flesh from his back and disfigure his dear face beyond recognition? Can you feel her breaking heart as she stood beneath that cross watching them callously drive the nails through those precious hands she had taught to hold a cup, those feet she had taught to walk? Can you hear her cry out to God with a mother's desperate plea to let her bear some of this awful suffering for her child?

Yet there is nothing recorded there of her rebellion. Just as she had accepted the angel's announcement about his birth, she accepted her son's death on behalf of mankind, though her soul must have writhed in agony with every blow.

Worse, she probably did not fully understand what was happening until after the resurrection, when she and her other sons became worshippers of this one they had known so well, yet had not known at all.

Nevertheless, Mary did not need to ask why. She knew. It was for this purpose that she had endured the birth pangs in that stable thirty-three years before. She had not realized what terrible things her son would have to endure, but she had known from the beginning that it would require something extraordinary to be the Savior of the world.

MICHAL

Not every Bible woman knew that same sweet response to the pains and disappointments of life. When King Saul's beautiful young daughter, Michal, fell in love with David, Saul was delighted. Jealous of David's popularity with the people, the king saw Michal's love as a trap for the young warrior. "I will let her marry David. Then she will be a trap for him, and the Philistines will defeat him" (1 Sam. 18:21 NCV).

David, though, with Michal's help, escaped trap after trap set by the murderous Saul. To show his appreciation for his wife's loyalty, the love of her youth left her behind in her father's palace. Her loving father spitefully and callously married her off to another man (1 Sam. 25:44).

After her father's death, David demanded Michal's return. By then, she had been married for ten years to her second husband—perhaps happily, for the man adored her and followed after her, weeping, when David took her back.

Did David suddenly realize how much he loved and missed

Michal, after all those years of accumulating wives and concubines and indulging in affairs? No, he needed the daughter of Saul as his wife for political reasons as he assumed her father's throne, and Michal knew it.

Cynical and bitter at the way she had been used by both her father and David, the last straw for Michal was when she looked out the palace window and saw her husband leaping and dancing at the head of a parade in his underwear, to the delight of the slave girls. Second Samuel 6:16 says she "despised him in her heart."

"When David returned home to bless his household, Michal daughter of Saul came out to meet him and said, 'How the king of Israel has distinguished himself today, disrobing in the sight of the slave girls of his servants as any vulgar fellow would'" (2 Sam. 6:20).

Who could blame Michal for growing bitter? She had been used and abused by the two men in her life whom she should have been able to trust. However, she allowed her bitterness toward her father and her husband to come between her and God, and cut herself off from the blessings he may have had in store for her. The story ends with what was considered a great curse in those days: "And Michal daughter of Saul had no children to the day of her death" (2 Sam. 6:23).

BACK TO MARY

Mary's reaction to the bitter cup she was given to drink was different from Michal's. The Bible tells us little of her feelings as she witnessed the terrible scenes leading to her Son's death, but bitterness seems to have been as far removed from her nature as rebellion.

Donna, too, though fearful of what lay ahead of her unsaved son as he went to war, was not bitter. She knew God was in control and trusted that he had Todd's eternal welfare in mind. She would pray that her son would be one of those saved in a foxhole on the battlefield, or that some chaplain or service buddy would be able to convince him of his need for salvation.

Donna and I still pray that her son will be saved, but he did come home safely when his foreign mission was completed, as Mary's did.

No, God did not spare Mary's son the cross. He could not, or we all would be lost. Nevertheless, Mary lived to see her precious son again, alive and well for eternity. Perhaps her story continued something like this.

A new kind of bird was singing in the tree beside the well. She wished Jesus were here to identify it for her and tell her of its habits. She sorely missed his stories, his deep understanding of how things in nature illustrated *Yahweh's* deeper truths. "The birds neither sow nor reap," he had pointed out, "yet their heavenly father feeds them. The lilies do not toil or spin, and yet not even Solomon in all his glory was arrayed like one of these."

She understood that he meant she should not worry, for *Yahweh* would provide for their needs. It was an obvious lesson in faith.

Sometimes, though, he spoke in parables that seemed to have a deeper meaning concealed inside the obvious one. Once, when they were planting the wheat that would supply the flour for their bread, he had stood with that far-off look in his eyes, rolling one of the kernels between his fingers. "Unless a kernel of wheat falls to the ground and dies," he had mused, "it remains only a single seed. But if it dies, it produces many seeds."

She was sure there was more to this simple statement than a prediction of the harvest, but when she asked him what it meant, he had assured her that she would "see and know" when the time was right.

She hadn't seen Jesus for some time, but she had heard the rumors about him. She had been told that, when he was baptized by John in the Jordan, as he came up out of the water, a white dove descended from heaven and settled on his shoulder and a voice cried out, "This is my beloved Son, in whom I am well pleased."

After his baptism, Jesus had disappeared into the wilderness for many days. When he had emerged, his brothers said he was changed, that there was a new authority about him and that he performed unbelievable miracles. James swore he had fed thousands from only five small loaves and two fish, and that there had been baskets of food remaining when they had eaten their fill. Simon said he went about healing the sick, casting out demons. He even had raised the dead, if the rumors were to be believed.

Why should I doubt any of it? she thought. *Is he not the Son of* Yahweh, *come to Earth in human form?*

Perhaps she did not want to fully understand what it meant to be the Son of God in human form, to have the daunting task of saving his people from their sins. Perhaps she preferred to see him simply as her beloved firstborn, following in her husband's footsteps as a carpenter, coming home at night to eat hungrily of the meal she had prepared for him, talking with her of ordinary things from an ordinary day.

She knew, though, that he had moved beyond all that now. The crowds followed him, eager to hear his amazing teachings and be the recipients of his miracles. He was in danger of being swallowed up by them. She had let her other sons persuade her to go with them to search out Jesus and try to get him to restrain himself.

"He claimed in a synagogue to be *haMeshiach,* and the congregation tried to throw him off a cliff," Simon reported. "He is going to get himself killed. But he will listen to you, *Imah,* if he will listen to anybody."

He hadn't, though. When his followers had told him that his mother and brothers wanted to speak with him, he had responded, "Who is my mother and who are my brothers?" Then, he had turned to the crowd and said, "My mother and brothers are those who hear God's word and put it into practice."

Mary knew her sons had been furious to be rejected so by their elder brother, but she thought she understood what Jesus meant. He was distancing himself from earthly ties and acknowledging heavenly ones. He surely was "about his Father's business," as he had warned them he must be when he was twelve.

Still, she was afraid for him. He had stirred up the anger of the Jewish leaders when he called them "a generation of vipers" and "white-washed sepulchers." The Pharisees, she heard, were plotting to kill him. She sighed deeply, knowing there was nothing she could do to protect this child of her heart. His purpose for coming into this world must be fulfilled. All she could do was submit to the will of *Yahweh,* as always, and watch what happened.

Yahweh *protected Daniel from the lions. He delivered Hananiah, Mishael, and Azariah from the fiery furnace. Surely he will protect this Son of his from the Sadducees and Pharisees, and from the mob that threatens to overwhelm him.*

She knew what was to come would not be easy. Had not old Simeon warned her that day when they had taken Jesus to the temple to fulfill the customs of the Law for the newborn? "This child is destined to cause the falling and rising of many in Israel," the old man had prophesied, "and to be a sign that will be spoken against, so that the thoughts of many hearts will be revealed. And a sword will pierce your own soul, too." She had tried not to think about those words, but they were carved in her mind like etchings on stone. She could not forget....

"*Imah.* Come quickly," James called, running toward her. "We must go to Jerusalem. They have arrested Jesus and are taking him before the Sanhedrin."

Mary caught her breath. *Whatever is to be required of him,* she thought with dread, *it has begun.*

Mary sat on a bench in the gardens behind John's house, her hands folded idly in her lap. John and his family had tried to comfort her, but their kind words could not penetrate her numb mind. Instead she kept hearing over and over the agonized cry, *"Eli, Eli, lama sabachthani?"* ["My God, my God, why have you forsaken me?"] Then, in the midst of his agony, he had cried out for God to forgive his tormentors.

"Mary, you must eat something," John urged gently, coming toward her with a bowl in his hands. She looked at the food and felt nausea rising in her throat. *Why?* she wanted to cry. *I must eat only if I want to go on living.*

John leaned closer. "The psalm tells us, dear Mother, that 'Weeping may remain for a night, but rejoicing comes in the morning.'"

She stared at him blankly. *Rejoicing?* She couldn't imagine ever rejoicing again.

John patted her on the shoulder, set the bowl on the bench beside her, and went sorrowfully back inside the house.

She knew she should show more appreciation for the kindness John and his family had shown her ever since Jesus had called down to them from the cross, "John, behold your mother. Mother, behold your son." In his pain he had thought of her and asked his best friend to consider her as his own mother.

Since they laid him in that borrowed tomb, she had been here, obediently accompanying them inside as darkness fell, sipping the strong-tasting brews they handed her, falling into exhausted sleep for a few hours.

When she awoke, it was to see again his poor disfigured face, looking at her with love and concern from eyes battered and torn beyond recognition. She closed her eyes, but could not shut out the sight.

"Oh, *Yahweh,*" she cried silently, "How precious he was, how special. How I have loved him."

She was not bitter toward *Yahweh.* She was just bruised—not in body, as poor Jesus had been, but in mind and spirit. All the years of his growing up, if she had known how it would end, she was sure she could not have endured it. *Yahweh* had been merciful in hiding it from her.

"I still don't understand, *Adonai,*" she whispered, "but I know I must accept your will, as he did." She had heard him pray more than once, "Not my will, but yours be done."

"Mary! Mary! Come quickly!" John's voice interrupted her thoughts as he ran toward her. "He is risen! He is risen, just as he said he would, only we did not understand until now."

The incredible words pushed through the fog of pain in Mary's brain, and she rose to her feet. She looked into John's eyes with doubt-shadowed hope.

John took both her hands in his. "Mary," he said earnestly, "the stone has been rolled away, and I have seen the empty tomb with my own eyes. I have touched the discarded grave clothes. He is risen, I tell you. Come and see the place where he lay. He is not there."

Joy spread through her as John's words registered in her mind. *Oh,* Yahweh, *forgive me,* she prayed silently. *I have trusted you all my life, but I let the despair of these past hours blind me to your truth.*

"It is finished!" he had cried just before he died. She had

thought he was referring to his death, but now she knew he was declaring that he had completed the work he had been sent into the world to do. *The price has been paid. Those horrible hours on that barbaric cross, and those leading up to it, his poor broken body and spilled blood were what it took to save his people from their sins.* He had tried to tell her, but like John, she had not understood until now.

"Unless a kernel of wheat fall to the ground and die, it remains a single seed," he had said. "But if it dies, it produces many seeds." He had known he was to be that grain of wheat, dying and being raised to new life, making it possible for all who believe in him to have life, also.

"Of course he is risen," she said with new assurance, taking the arm John offered her. "Don't you see, John?" she said, smiling up at him, "Not only has he saved his people from their sins, but he has conquered death as well."

First Peter 3:18 says: "For Christ died for sins once for all, the righteous for the unrighteous, to bring you to God. He was put to death in the body but made alive by the Spirit." It was his resurrection that changed the crucifixion of Jesus from merely the untimely death of a good man to the ultimate triumph over sin and death. When he came out of that tomb, even Satan knew the game was over. It was "Allie, allie, all in free" for all who believe.

YOU, ME, AND JOHN THE BAPTIST

John the Baptist was in prison, facing execution. It would be safe to say he was in a desperate situation. Doubt crept into his mind. He remembered the dove that had sat on Jesus' shoulder and the voice from heaven saying, "This is my beloved Son." But if his cousin truly was the Messiah, why hadn't he delivered him from prison and death?

He sent two of his disciples to ask Jesus, "Are you the one who was to come, or should we expect someone else?" (Luke 7:19).

Jesus sent them back to John with the message: "The blind receive sight, the lame walk, those who have leprosy are cured, the deaf hear, the dead are raised, and the good news is preached to the poor" (Luke 7:22).

232 / TIMELESS *needs*, ETERNAL *hope*

John was reassured that the Savior had come. He still had not been delivered from his situation, but he knew that, no matter how desperate the circumstances, God was in control.

He still is. Despite the cries of doom from the media and certain misguided politicians, we are not going to burn up from global warming. We are not going to see our world destroyed by a meteor crashing into the ocean. We are not going to see planting time and harvest disappear from the earth (Gen. 8:22).

IF YOU'RE STILL DESPERATE ...

Maybe your current need is different from any of the desperate situations we have explored in this book. Whatever your circumstances, remember: God loves you. He knows your name. He knew you as you were being knit together in your mother's womb. He saw you when you cut that first tooth and when you lost it. He watched you grow up in that loving home, or saw the pain and anguish you endured as you were neglected or abused.

About now you're probably saying, "If he loves me so much, why has he let these terrible things happen to me?"

Why *do* bad things happen to good people? Why is Sally strong and healthy, while Elaine battles heart disease and Wilma is disabled with fibromyalgia? Why is Marilyn adored and pampered by her husband, while Jane, through no fault of her own, is battered and bruised by hers? Why were Sean and Lisa born into homes where they are comfortable, well-fed, and cherished, while young Sam is cold, hungry, and unloved, and little Katie is sexually abused?

Why do the innocent suffer? Why did God allow those awful things in your life? Why are you still facing this desperate situation?

All we know for sure is that life is filled with troubles. Some of these we bring on ourselves through unwise choices, but others seem to fall on us out of the sky for no reason.

Jesus was the Son of God born into humanity, and the only human being ever to live a sinless life. Yet he was despised and rejected, misunderstood, treated unfairly, accused of being mad or demon-possessed. He was mocked, spit upon, beaten, and crucified. When it comes to suffering, he has "been there, done that, and got the T-shirt." One thing is certain: Jesus can understand and empathize with any desperate situation we may be enduring.

God does not create evil, though he sometimes allows things to come into our lives, as he did with Job, that we may not understand until we see the whole picture from his viewpoint. But I've learned that he never allows anything to come into my life without a purpose. Usually, he has several, and—whether or not I like it—they all are aimed at making me the kind of person he can stand to have around for eternity.

IF YOU'RE EXPECTING SMOOTH SAILING ...

Perhaps you're thinking, *I've accepted God's plan of salvation and made his son, Jesus, the Lord of my life. The Holy Spirit guides my steps. I will never experience pain or sorrow again.*

Wrong. I've had more pain and sorrow in my life, many more attacks of Satan since I accepted Jesus as my Savior and Lord than I endured before that life-changing event.

You see, Satan doesn't care how much religion we have. He just laughs at our pious demeanor and our busy work. He loves it when we bore some Sunday-school class with our stale repetition of an outdated lesson that has no relevance to today's living. He doesn't care how many pews we warm or how many church socials we attend. He doesn't even care if we bring the beans and the slaw.

He is, however, scared to death of our truly understanding John 3:16, of our finding out how much God loves, not only the world, but each of us, up close and personal. He will do everything in his power to keep us from forming a personal relationship with Jesus Christ.

IF YOU'RE EXPECTING GOD'S DELIVERANCE ...

Will God deliver you from this current desperate situation? Maybe. Maybe not. But you can be assured that he will go with you through it, and that what the devil meant for evil, God, somehow, will turn into good. Romans 8:28 tells us, "And we know that in all things God works for the good of those who love him."

That's one of those unbreakable "If you will, then I will" promises. It means if I love him, he will be there for me. It means, if you make him the center of your life, he will bring you through this desperate situation—and the next, and the next. Why? Because he loves us so much that he died for us.

READERS' GUIDE

This book takes a deeper look at ten women from the Bible—along with some of their modern counterparts—and the desperate situations in which they found themselves. It attempts to show how God hears and answers the cry of a desperate woman and provides solutions for her needs, if she will let him.

Chapter 1 — Bathsheba

In this chapter we gave Bathsheba and Justine the benefit of the doubt and assumed they just happened to be in the wrong place at the wrong time, like Humpty-Dumpty, and had not deliberately set out to sin.

What poor choices did Bathsheba and Justine make that contributed to the desperate situations in which they later found themselves?

What could Bathsheba and Justine have done to prevent what happened to them?

How can someone who is suffering guilt because of the results of bad choices find peace?

Why is it harder to forgive ourselves than to forgive someone else?

If someone came to you and confessed that she was pregnant by her boss, a married man who had threatened to fire her from a much-needed job if she did not have sex with him, what would your reaction be? Would you turn away from her in disgust, as Uriah had every right to do with Bathsheba? Or would you try to help her? If so, how?

CHAPTER 2 — THE PRODIGAL'S MOTHER

This imagined story of the mother of the legendary Prodigal Son deals with perseverance, with never giving up hope as we seek to bring our lost loved ones to Christ.

If you have a lost son or daughter, like Tikvah or Joanne and I, and you've scattered those solid "pebbles" from God's Word throughout their growing-up years, you've cautioned them to seek a relationship with their Creator through the sacrifice of his Son, Jesus, what more can you do?

Or it may be that the one whose salvation is of such concern to you is a brother or sister, a dear aunt, a cherished grandfather, a cousin, or friend. You weren't there to plant those spiritual path-markers in their early years. You have tried to witness to them in later life, but it just hasn't seemed to make an impact. What else can you do?

Why is it so difficult to win those you love the most to the Lord?

At what point do we just give up and let them suffer the consequences of their own decisions? What insight have you gained from this chapter about perseverance?

If we give up on winning a loved one to Christ, can we expect God not to give up on them?

CHAPTER 3 — GOMER

In our study of the hedonistic Gomer, Loretta, and Peter Rabbit, we looked at the deliberate choice of a life of sin over a more respectable and God-pleasing lifestyle.

What difference do you see in the unintentional sins of a
Bathsheba and the deliberate sins of a Gomer?

How do they compare with the self-centered Loretta who
acknowledges God, but is indifferent to him and makes no
place for him in her life?

Is there a difference in the power of the sins of these three women
to separate them from God? Does one sinner need a savior
more than another?

Is someone you love in danger of slipping into one of these three
   categories—the unintentional sinner, the deliberate sinner, or
   the indifferent sinner? What can you do to prevent it?

When you examine your own life, what characteristics do you
   find that remind you of Bathsheba, Gomer, or Loretta? What
   should you do about that?

CHAPTER 4 — HANNAH

As we looked at Hannah and Megan, we saw that commitment
must be honored, even when it hurts.

What would you do if you were in a similar situation as Hannah
   or Megan? Could you endure the wondering about where the
   child was, if she was being cared for properly, if he was happy
   and well?

Have you ever made a hasty commitment and then found that it was going to hurt desperately to keep it? What did you do?

Have you ever made a commitment that, for some reason, you could not keep? How did you feel about it? In hindsight what would you have done differently if you could?

Have you come to terms with your decision? If necessary, have you asked God to forgive you and been restored to fellowship with him?

Have you forgiven yourself?

CHAPTER 5 — REBEKAH

In this chapter we explored the consequences of the determination of Rebekah and Macbeth to control the events of their lives. In each case a prediction was made, and they set out to ensure that it came to pass, without seeking God's guidance or favor.

Why didn't Rebekah and Macbeth wait for God to bring about these desired events?

What did Macbeth's ruthless actions cost him?

What did Rebekah's lies and deception cost her?

Is there something in your life that you want to happen more than anything? What will you do if God says no?

Are you already impatiently running ahead of God, trying to
  bring your desire to fruition? How do you think God would
  prefer you handle the situation?

CHAPTER 6 — ABIGAIL

Sometimes, like Abigail and Ellen, we are forced to fill roles and
undertake duties God never intended for us as women. When the
men in our lives either refuse or neglect these responsibilities, we
often must step in and see that these essential tasks are done.

If you have to fulfill the role of head of household for your family, are you becoming bitter about it? Do you find yourself
  being publicly critical of your mate because of your disappointments in him? What can you do to make your attitude
  line up with the Word of God?

If you are single—never married, widowed, or divorced—and

have no other choice but to be head of your household, has this chapter enabled you to see that being married does not always provide a woman with someone who will accept his God-given role as head-of-household? How does knowing that there are many married women who are struggling with the same role you must play as a single woman reduce your feelings that life isn't fair?

What are some ways you can fill this unwanted role without "stressing out" or succumbing to despair?

If your husband is properly leading your household in its relationship with God, do you show him that you appreciate his efforts? Or do you struggle for the dominant role? What changes do you need to make in this area?

Examine your attitude and actions in the head-of-household role. How well do they line up with the Word of God? What do you need to do differently?

CHAPTER 7 — JOB'S WIFE

We learned with Mrs. Job, Laura, and Darrell that sometimes there just is no explanation for why God causes or allows some things to come into our lives.

Do you believe God sends illness, financial ruin, or other dire circumstances on people as punishment for sin? Why or why not?

Have you had to surrender someone dear to the Lord's will, even though you prayed diligently for his or her healing? What are your feelings about it?

Through no recognizable fault of your own, have you suffered some devastating personal loss, other than the death of a loved one, that has left you bitter and depressed?

How can you encourage someone who is questioning the terrible things going on in his or her life, when the last few times you prayed there seemed to be no answer, or the answer was a flat no?

Have you, like Job, come to the place where you accept the right of the Creator to do what he will with his creation? Have you reached the point where you can surrender to his authority and simply say, "Though he slay me, yet will I trust him!"? If not, how can you work through your present feelings to a new relationship with the Lord?

CHAPTER 8 — THE INNKEEPER'S WIFE

In this chapter we met the hypothetical Deborah and her modern counterpart, Alice, and looked at a woman's need to be appreciated, to be special. Like the Velveteen Rabbit, we all want to be *Real*, to know that we are important to someone, not because of what we can do for them, but just because of who we are.

Do you feel that if you disappeared from the face of the earth no one would notice?

Do you seek identity in the value placed upon you by someone else? How much of your self-esteem is based on how others see you?

How does knowing that Jesus looked on you with enough love to die for you change your estimation of your self-worth?

Make a list of things you long to try—a new job or hobby, a different style of clothing or hairdo, an exciting new relationship. What can you do to gather up the courage to reach out for any of them?

List the things you feel are your shortcomings on the left side of a sheet of paper and your obvious good qualities on the right. What can you do to improve or get rid of those things listed on the left? What can you do to take full advantage of those things in the right column?

CHAPTER 9 — LYDIA

In this chapter we saw that God is always looking out for widows like Lydia and Grace.

Why do you think the Bible stresses the fact that widows and orphans hold a special place in God's heart?

If you are a widow—or close to someone who is—think about the ways everyday physical or financial needs have been met since widowhood began. What things seem to be direct interventions of God?

Have you turned to God when the lonely nights seem never-
ending or when the house echoes with emptiness and felt his
warmth enfold you? If not, why not?

Have you discovered, like Grace, that becoming involved in other
people's problems takes your mind off your own troubles?
Name some instances where this has been so.

If you are not currently a widow, without being morbid or fatalis-
tic, how can you prepare for the eventuality that you may
someday have to live alone?

CHAPTER 10 — MARY

We have looked at Mary here simply as a human mother who loved her special child with all her heart. We have shared her joy in her extraordinary son, and plumbed the depths of her pain as she watched his incredible sufferings.

Can you remember a time when you had to watch your innocent child suffer—from a bee sting, a toothache, an illness, an accident—and longed to bear at least part of his pain?

Perhaps there was a time when you had to watch your not-so-innocent child (or other loved one) suffer the consequences of his/her own actions. How did you feel about the suffering of the guilty party?

How did your reactions to your child's suffering—whether guilty or innocent—compare to Mary's?

Have you, like Donna, had to send a lost son (or daughter) off to war, or into some other danger, knowing that if he were killed, he would spend eternity in hell? How did your own reactions compare to Donna's?

What have you learned from Mary that might help you handle your own desperate situations in a way more pleasing to God?

YOU, ME, AND JOHN THE BAPTIST

John the Baptist learned that, though his world had turned upside down, God was in control. Still, John lost his head!

How can you explain bad things happening to good people, despite God being in control?

Why do you think God has allowed so much pain and turmoil in
your life?

If you pray hard enough, will God take away your pain, illness,
trouble? Will he reverse that financial disaster you are facing
or change your rebellious prodigal to a loving and obedient
child?

In the accounts given in the New Testament, while he was here
on earth, Jesus never refused to answer the pleas of all who
sought his help. If his power is undiminished or enhanced
since he went back to heaven, if distance and time have no
effect on him, why do so many of our prayers seem to bounce
off the ceiling? Why are there so many desperate situations
today?

Why doesn't God explain the purpose for our suffering when it
would make it so much easier to bear?

It has been said that someday, when we view the proverbial "tapestry" of our lives from the upper side, we will be able to see the beautiful pattern God has woven from all the bits and pieces we have seen from this side. Perhaps right now, Darrell understands, at last, why God allowed all that suffering in his life. Perhaps he and Job, and maybe even John the Baptist, are agreeing that their present glory was worth it all.

Someday we, too, will understand the good we enjoyed and the bad we endured during our lifetimes. Right now all we can know for sure is what it says in Romans 8:28: "... in all things God works for the good of those who love him ..." In other words, he always has our best interests in mind.